MIKE BARTLETT

Mike Bartlett is a multi-award-winning playwright and screenwriter.

His plays include *Scandaltown* (Lyric Hammersmith, London); *The 47th* (The Old Vic, London/Sonia Friedman Productions/ Annapurna Theatre); *Mrs Delgado* (Arts at the Old Fire Station, Oxford/Theatre Royal Bath/Oxford Playhouse), *Snowflake* (Arts at the Old Fire Station/Kiln Theatre, London); *Albion* (Almeida Theatre, London, also filmed for BBC Four); *Wild* (Hampstead Theatre, London); *Game* (Almeida); *King Charles III* (Almeida/ West End/Broadway; Critics' Circle Award for Best New Play, Olivier Award for Best New Play, Tony Award nomination for Best Play); *An Intervention* (Paines Plough/ Watford Palace Theatre); *Bull* (Sheffield Theatres/Young Vic Theatre, London/ Off-Broadway; TMA Best New Play Award, Olivier Award for Outstanding Achievement in an Affiliate Theatre); *Medea* (Glasgow Citizens/Headlong/Watford Palace); *Chariots of Fire* (based on the film; Hampstead/West End); *13* (National Theatre, London); *Love, Love, Love* (Paines Plough/Plymouth Drum/ Royal Court Theatre, London; TMA Best New Play Award); *Earthquakes in London* (Headlong/National Theatre); *Cock* (Royal Court/Off-Broadway, Olivier Award for Outstanding Achievement in an Affiliate Theatre; revived in the West End); *Artefacts* (nabokov/Bush Theatre, London); *Contractions* and *My Child* (Royal Court).

Bartlett has received BAFTA nominations for his television series *The Town* (ITV) and *Doctor Foster* (Drama Republic/ BBC), for which he won Outstanding Newcomer for British Television Writing at the British Screenwriters' Awards 2016. His screen adaptation of his play *King Charles III* aired on BBC Two in 2017, and his other television series include *Life* (BBC One), *Sticks and Stones* and *Trauma* (both Tall Story Pictures for ITV), and *Press* (Lookout Point for BBC One). Bartlett has also written several plays for radio, winning the Writers' Guild Tinniswood and Imison Prizes for *Not Talking*.

Mike Bartlett

The 47th

NICK HERN BOOKS

London

www.nickhernbooks.co.uk

A Nick Hern Book

The 47th first published in Great Britain in 2022 as a paperback original by Nick Hern Books Limited, The Glasshouse, 49a Goldhawk Road, London W12 8QP

The 47th copyright © 2022 Mike Bartlett

Mike Bartlett has asserted his right to be identified as the author of this work

Cover image: iStock.com/Willard

Designed and typeset by Nick Hern Books, London
Printed in Great Britain by Mimeo Ltd, Huntingdon, Cambridgeshire PE29 6XX

A CIP catalogue record for this book is available from the British Library

ISBN 978 1 83904 074 0

Woodland CARBON
www.woodlandcarbon.co.uk
NICK HERN BOOKS
Printed on Carbon Captured paper

The 47th was first produced by The Old Vic, Sonia Friedman Productions and Annapurna Theatre at The Old Vic, London, on 29 March 2022, with the following cast:

DONALD TRUMP	Bertie Carvel
KAMALA HARRIS	Tamara Tunie
IVANKA TRUMP	Lydia Wilson
ENSEMBLE	David Carr
SHAMAN	Joss Carter
CHARLIE TAKAHASHI	James Cooney
ENSEMBLE	Charles Craddock
ENSEMBLE	Flora Dawson
ENSEMBLE	Eva Fontaine
TED CRUZ / BILL CLINTON / PAUL	James Garnon
STEVE RICHETTI / OHIO SENATOR	Richard Hansell
ENSEMBLE	Miya James
DONALD JUNIOR / MATT	Oscar Lloyd
HEIDI CRUZ / MODERATOR / CIA	Jenni Maitland
ERIC TRUMP	Freddie Meredith
BARACK OBAMA / GENERAL TAYLOR	Ben Onwukwe
TINA FLOURNOY / NURSE VITA	Cherrelle Skeete
GEORGE W. BUSH / ENSEMBLE	David Tarkenter
ROSIE TAKAHASHI	Ami Tredrea
JOE BIDEN	Simon Williams

All other parts played by members of the company

Director	Rupert Goold
Set	Miriam Buether
Costume	Evie Gurney
Lighting	Neil Austin

Sound	Tony Gayle
Original Music and Sound Score	Adam Cork
Video	Ash J Woodward
Movement	Lynne Page
Wigs, Hair and Make-up	Richard Mawbey
Casting	Jessica Ronane CDG
US Casting	Jim Carnahan CSA
Voice	Joel Trill
Dialect	Brett Tyne
Associate Director	Sara Aniqah Malik
Associate Set	Alex Berry
Costume Supervisor	Zoë Thomas-Webb
Props Supervisor	Lizzie Frankl and Fahmida Bakht for Propworks
Company Stage Manager	Dan Ayling
Deputy Stage Manager	Lorna Seymour
Assistant Stage Manager	Emily Ida

The 47th was an Old Vic, Sonia Friedman Productions and Annapurna Theatre co-production.

The production was brought to The Old Vic in collaboration with Fictional Company and Almeida Theatre.

Characters

DEMOCRATS
VICE-PRESIDENT HARRIS
PRESIDENT BIDEN
STEVE RICHETTI
CHARLIE TAKAHASHI
TINA FLOURNOY
BARACK OBAMA
GEORGE W. BUSH
BILL CLINTON
SPEECHWRITER

REPUBLICANS
DONALD J. TRUMP
IVANKA TRUMP
ERIC TRUMP
DONALD TRUMP JR
TED CRUZ
HEIDI CRUZ
ROSIE TAKAHASHI
OHIO SENATOR
PAUL
DAVE
SOLDIER

THE MODERATOR
HEAD OF THE FBI
HEAD OF THE CIA
VITA
MATT

Plus SENATORS, CONGRESSMEN, SOLDIERS,
SECURITY, ATTENDANTS, CROWDS, ARMED GUARDS,
OFFICIALS, AIDES

Note on Text

(/) means the next speech begins at that point.

(–) means the next line interrupts.

(…) at the end of a speech means it trails off. On its own it indicates a pressure, expectation or desire to speak.

A line with no full stop at the end indicates that the next speech follows on immediately.

This text went to press before the end of rehearsals and so may differ slightly from the play as performed.

ACT ONE

1.1

Mar-a-Lago.

TRUMP *arrives on a golf buggy. Dismounts.*

TRUMP.
    I know, I know. You hate me. So much right?
    My face, this hair, my wife, you loathe the way
    I hold my hand, when making points. My lips?
    And even though you're all so liberal,
    You judge me by the colour of my skin!
    Not cool. Not cool. Just unbelievable
    But it's okay, I like a tan, I do.
    And hey, your hate is real, and beautiful.
    It's special hate, it makes you pure,
    And yet, you just can't get enough of me.
    You scan what I've done next, like slowing down
    In traffic 'Where's the blood? The severed head?
    I'm shocked, it's gross!' But you can't turn away.
    You all adore my entertainment.
    And more than *that*! It's not just fun you want,
    Because although I fib (I do, a bit),
    It's through this muddy fiction that I find
    The richest of commodities: The truth.
    You all proclaim your proscribed slogans, keen
    To show you're allies, 'Oh yes sir! Me too!'
    But those progressive mouths stay strangely closed
    In moments when your far more honest hearts
    Are telling you with clarity, this isn't right!
    The white men in the audience, you know
    Just how it feels when you are told without
    Connection to an action or a word
    With no regard to anything you've done
    It's slam! You're racist! Blam! Forget a judge,
    The proof of guilt's the pallor of your skin.

And we all know there's something wrong with that
But you don't want to say it. Sure. Well that's okay,
Cos here I am: Your devil. Oven-hot
And hot to trot with seventy-eight years done
And little left to lose.
We'll have some fun tonight, for I have plans
And plots aplenty, death and life and love
And gorgeous girls and men in pricey suits.
So eat your popcorn, settle down, listen hard
And watch, forget your heart, instead give me
Your gut (that's if you even have one left
You democratic motherfucking cunts).
Cos yes we're talking hate, not yours but mine
Of those that forced me from my rightful house.
To four years lonely exile here, four years
I can't afford, while they triumphant, laugh.
They'll rue their acts and suffer to the end
Behold as I commence my just revenge.

Enter IVANKA, DONALD TRUMP JR., *and* ERIC. DON
JR *with papers*.

DON JR.
  Hey Dad

TRUMP.
      Hey Don.

DON JR.
          You see? I shaved my beard.
  I think it takes ten years straight off! I'm told
  Without it people might by accident
  Take me for you, but thirty years ago.

IVANKA.
  Er no.

TRUMP.
      Who told you that?

DON JR.
              Was Kimberley

TRUMP.
Without your beard you look – I'd say – diffuse?
Because you have no chin, whilst I am blessed
By bones with structure you would not believe.
All from my father, in fact good looks were all
He gave me.

DON JR.
But the millions in loans?
And contacts, housing, backroom staff.

TRUMP.
It had
His strings attached. No, nothing came for free.
But here, the point is, I looked *good*. For gaze
Upon my face in Home Alone, or Zoolander
As I have done so many times, and see
That there amongst the sexy guys and girls
Of Hollywood, I hold my own amidst that pantheon.

IVANKA.
But Dad are you okay?

DON JR.
He's good, but needs
To sign these documents –

TRUMP.
Has Eric gone to sleep?

IVANKA.
He finds it hard
To stay awake without a visual stimulus

TRUMP.
Too much pornography no doubt, hey son!

ERIC.
Oh Father there you are, I had a dream.

TRUMP.
That's very sweet. But now before my own
Attention wanes, let's speak 'bout why I called
You here. For I've been thinking hard upon
My legacy. To whom I'll leave it all.

Tradition would suggest I share myself
Between all three, in equal measure bound
With equal love. But that feels not aligned
With my philosophy: to find the art
Within the deal.
And so today we'll choose the path ahead
Just one alone will be my rightful heir
And I demand you earn it all right here:
My cash, my contacts and what's more: my love.
By now explaining why it's you that should
Deserve my patronage.

DON JR.

                 Explain? I'd thought it obvious

ERIC.
Just one?

TRUMP.
       Just one.

DON JR.
              Okay. Well, if we must,
As eldest I'll go first. Endowed your name
When you're unable to attend it's me
They want. Like you I work that crowd into
A frenzy. Blazing adoration at
The Trump who's standing there aloft.
When I begin to speak, they stare, and hang
On every word –

TRUMP.
(They cannot wait for me.)

DON JR.
Before too long the zealous clamour grows,
The thousands chanting out my name

TRUMP.
                    (My name.)

DON JR.
And just like you
My businesses have always grown and thrived,

I am your mirror, Father. Donald named
And Donald Trump in bloody nature too.

TRUMP.
Thanks mirror man. Who's next to sue?

ERIC.
Though second born I'm pleading safety first.
While you so rightly went ashore to halt
The tide of socialism I did keep
The ship afloat. And when you came aboard
Again to look upon your treasured works,
Entrusted to my hands four years before,
You said to me, and these your very words:
I'd 'done okay'.

TRUMP.
              You did okay.

ERIC.
                        'Okay'.
From you the highest compliment indeed.
I've watched all fourteen seasons of your show
And none of your contestants make my match.
So look: You've got your real Apprentice here.
And oh what luck! He proudly bears your name.

TRUMP.
Presenting as a safety net? That's bold.
And now my gorgeous girl, what can you say
To roundly trump your siblings' pitch? Speak.

IVANKA.
Nothing, Father.

TRUMP.
Nothing?

IVANKA.
Nothing.

TRUMP.
Well Jesus sweetheart play the game at least.
It's not like you to coyly act the mute

To shyly duck your head and like a kid
Who cannot hit a ball, decide the game's
The fraud and not his fat-assed loser self.
(Don't get me wrong your ass is something else)

IVANKA.
If as my father you know not my love
Then words will not identify your daughter.
Your rightful heir will never beg, but trade.
You know my talent, and my promise too.
I'm grateful for all that you have bestowed
And vow that I'll repay that loan not just
In full but with my share of interest.

A moment.

TRUMP.
And just like that the mic is roundly dropped.
As if it would be any other way,
She had no competition. But don't worry.
You'll never go without, as long as all
Your loyalty flows, as now, in my direction.
And in good time of course, to her. Okay?

Beat.

DON JR.
For you she always was the brightest star.
We'll be content, mere planets orbiting
In her reflected glare.

ERIC.
Yeah me as well. I'm not a natural lead.

DON JR *and* ERIC *go*.

TRUMP.
And so my girl, it all comes down to you.
And what say you to that?

IVANKA.
I'm flattered by the role, but wonder why
You chose today to organise your state?
Did something happen?

TRUMP.

No. A Sadness creeps.
He's always been there I suppose, but now
He comes accompanying me to golf each day.
Where once trim birdie blew him to the wind
These days, for eighteen holes, he whispers, gloats
'Man once you were the club, so tall and lean,
You'd take the swing, then slip back in amongst
Your pals, each one so smooth and keenly honed.
Now look, dear Don, for you've become the ball
Endimpled, small, and yes still placed upon
A pedestal, but not these days to be
Adored but just to make you easier
To smack. And reeling thus, with no control,
You head towards the dark and blackest hole.'
And so this morning I decided if
I'm truly done, then now –

IVANKA.

But Dad, you're not –

Enter ROSIE TAKAHASHI.

ROSIE.

Excuse me ma'am?

IVANKA.

Rosie, I'll need more time.

ROSIE *makes to go*.

But hey – Dad! This is my new driver. Rosie. She's quite
your fan.

ROSIE.

Oh sir. It's really an honour to meet you, Mr President. I've
been a huge supporter from the very beginning, I was there,
wanted you to get the nomination, sir, and what happened in
2020, they fucking stole that thing, pardon my language. I
know what they say, but we want you to run again, do you
think you will?

TRUMP.

What do they say?

ROSIE.
That you're old.

TRUMP.
Okay.

ROSIE.
Yesterday's news, you know. But you're only the same as
Biden when he ran.

TRUMP.
And that's very old Rosie.

ROSIE.
Well if you change your mind, we'll be right there, me, my
friends, and I bet a whole lot more, no matter what they say.

TRUMP.
I'm sure someone will come along in time,
That you can nail your colours to

ROSIE.
It's just a pleasure and privilege to be working for y'all.

TRUMP.
You're what makes this country great Rosie. Women like
you.

ROSIE.
Wow. I'll die happy now. Thank you. Thank you.

IVANKA.
(*Meaningfully.*) Thank *you*.

ROSIE *goes.* TRUMP *reflective.*

I know in recent days you're sadder than
You were, the heavy age more greatly felt.
But if you left the compound here and tripped
Amongst the Rosies you would find you're loved
Not only equal to the warmth you knew
But more, for having had old Biden squat
For all these years within his stolen house,
Commander-in-thief, a doddering damp'ning squib
Your own blue-collar crowd, now feel the thing
They miss, and crave your swift return.

TRUMP.

You think?

IVANKA.
I know!

Enter BUTLER.

BUTLER.
Excuse me sir, it's Mr Cruz.

IVANKA.
It's who?

TRUMP.
Yes send him in.

BUTLER *goes*.

(*To* IVANKA.)   Whenever 'Mr Cruz'
Is said, it always makes me wish I was
About to meet the Scientologist.
For I would rather watch a mission thought
Impossible with death-defying stunts
Than Ted's deluded caper heading straight
And slowly to the middle of the road.

IVANKA.
Agreed. So why's he come?

Enter TED CRUZ *and* ATTENDANTS.

CRUZ.
Dear Donald thanks indeed for welcoming
Us here, already we've had such a time

TRUMP.
Where's Heidi, surely she would like to meet
Her host?

CRUZ.
                Indeed she would, unfortunately
She feels a little sickly from the sun.

TRUMP.
This is your problem Ted, you never say
It like it is.

CRUZ.

      Alright
It's true, she's sworn that from that day when you
Did tweet an ugly photograph and say
You'd spill the beans about her mental health
That she would never spend a moment in
Your company.

TRUMP.

      But stay at my hotel?

IVANKA.

You look like you would like to rest, is it
The heat?

CRUZ.

      I'm fine, but sure, let's sit and talk

TRUMP.

These chairs were made bespoke for me last week.
They cast my ass for special comfort.
It means that I sit well while others squirm.
But why in Florida? Not for the sun.

CRUZ.

Well as you know, in all the primaries
I have the lead, the nomination's well
Within my grasp. But come election day
The pollsters claim it's still too close to call.
Now understandably, at such an age,
You don't desire the job yourself again
(In any case it's got too late to run.)
But still I guess you want some influence?
For me, I'd find to make the run secure,
A Trump card was the presidential seal.

TRUMP.

You ask for my endorsement Ted?

CRUZ.

      That's right.
I know we've had our disagreements but
I made your case in Congress even when
The other shirkers kissed you on both cheeks

Denied you thrice, impeached and happ'ly tried
To have you barred from ever going back.
Not me. Remember that.

TRUMP.

I do indeed.

CRUZ.

There can be no dispute, without your lead
Republicans would be a waning force.

TRUMP.

But you just said that you don't want my lead.
Instead I'm… what? A coach? A strong support?
Or maybe seeing as I'm blond and fit
You'll give me pompoms, pigtail too, and have
Me jumping up and down, gimme a 'T'
Then next an 'E' and finally 'D': It's Ted!

CRUZ.

Support whatever way you like but this
Is just to ask your help.

TRUMP.

I see.

CRUZ.

With us combined, my White House lies in wait.

Beat.

IVANKA.

Hey Dad, if I might talk with you alone?

TRUMP.

Ivanka why? For Mr Cruz is it!
Just as he said he's all but nominee.
Yes, Ted may not possess my thrills and spills
But honestly, who does? I'd rather own
A tiny piece of power here, than none
At all.

IVANKA.

These words are from your mouth, but still,
They don't sound like my father.

TRUMP.
Well age brings not just wisdom but humility.
The world that once was ours is passed along
To younger less exciting hands.

CRUZ.
                                    That's true.
Excitement's not perhaps my strength, but once
I have your blessing here, we can inject
A little of your spit and blood into
The arm of these United States. And like
A vaccine, just that dose will be enough
To stop the virus of the Democrats.

IVANKA.
Please Dad we ought –

TRUMP.
                          You are endorsed.

CRUZ.
                                        My thanks.

A moment. IVANKA *unhappy.*

TRUMP.
And please, you tell your wife from me.
It's good that she refused to see me here.
Unlike her husband she has lines she draws.
If trespassed on she builds a wall to shut
The perpetrator out, and in this way
She claims what you cannot: Integrity.

CRUZ.
We'll be in touch. Goodbye sir. Ivanka.

He goes.

TRUMP.
Ivanka, look! Your face like thunder claps.
Your father pledges his to someone else?
A tragedy! All hope has gone and life's
Unfair. But think of all you have. Your house.
Your wealth. Your friends and education too.
You owe it all to me. So give your trust.

Or if you don't, then check your rings in at
The desk. Go find the door. You're on the street.

IVANKA.
You know you'll always have my loyalty.

She goes.

TRUMP.
I've found when plotting, there's a golden rule
No better secret kept then one that stays
Within the tightly guarded mental vault.
Make silence fall, your flapping mouth tie down
With patience, it's your thoughts that seize the crown.

TRUMP *goes.*

1.2

Washington National Cathedral.

We see a suitable tribute photo of President Jimmy Carter.

A funeral cortège crosses the stage. Following it is
PRESIDENT BIDEN, *and the former presidents.* BIDEN *peels
off. With him, his chief-of-staff,* STEVE RICHETTI.

BIDEN.
For four score years and ten we had
A country free of plague. That's not far off
The length of time I've walked upon this earth.
And yet, when thrice attempt did prove a charm,
And finally my White House moment came,
It spread once more. So with a handshake and
A cough, my presidency's been defined
Before I even chose my wooden desk.

RICHETTI.
Well then what better reason do you need
Than, having won the race, and hearing full

Appreciation of the crowd, to turn
And jog back to the start to run again?

BIDEN.

                                        I want that but
The clock ticks loudly in my ear. The vast
Majority of friends not only are
Retired from their jobs, but from their lives.
The former president is one more gone.
Each day I wake and feel my blood is fresh
My body fit as ever was, my brain
Alert, I leap from bed, but heading to
The bathroom mirror I receive a shock.
For staring back at me's a travesty,
A horror of the man I dream each night.

HARRIS.
Hey Joe!

They turn as KAMALA HARRIS *enters with* TINA
FLOURNOY, *her chief-of-staff.*

                You know as I arrived I saw
This new young guy was striding up the aisle.

BIDEN.
Okay…

HARRIS.
        I thought him fresh to give advice,
Or act as bodyguard, but then he turned,
And he was not an aide at all, but you!
My God, it's getting weird!
Have you a picture in the White House attic?

BIDEN.
We've many pictures in the attic yes
For Donald chose a most offensive range
And once arrived we had them deeply stashed.
But none of them preserve this aged body,
You're kind but we must face the fact I'm old.

HARRIS.
But you're not on your own, you have your team
And dare I say there's mine as well, we all

Serve at the pleasure of the president
In fact we hope that in your second term
You might decide to give us slightly more
To do?

BIDEN.

Ah Kamala, I'm just advised
That with my age, if I used you too much
They'd claim I'm ill, or secretly had died.
Though... maybe that's a sign my time is up?
Perhaps my second term should be your first?

HARRIS.

Er – no. You won, not me. I am a pragmatist

RICHETTI.

And sir, you must decide, it's getting late.

Beat.

BIDEN.

Perhaps we wait another week?

RICHETTI.

No sir
We have already waited and each time –

BIDEN.

Aha! They're here.

BARACK OBAMA, GEORGE W. BUSH *and* BILL
CLINTON *enter. With them, a photographer. Also, journalist*
CHARLIE TAKAHASHI. BIDEN *goes to them and they
have their photograph taken.* CHARLIE *talks to* HARRIS.

HARRIS.

Hey Charlie, how are you?

CHARLIE.

I'm nervous, ma'am. I'm going on the road
With Cruz quite soon, and that feels like
Vacation next to this.

HARRIS.

I know, it's weird
To interview a single president would give me shakes,
But four?

CHARLIE.
Is there collective noun for presidents?

HARRIS.
An oval maybe?

CHARLIE.
Pride?

HARRIS.
A herd?

The PRESIDENTS *have finished and come down to meet* CHARLIE *and* HARRIS.

CLINTON.
Succession Kamala. We're a succession.
The past, the present and I see the ghost
Of future too.

HARRIS.
Oh Bill, you're kind but Joe's our guy.

(*Aside to* CHARLIE.) Shake not, there's no one better for the task.

(*To the others*.) I'll leave you to your talk.

HARRIS *leaves*.

CHARLIE.
Might I
Begin by asking of the qualities
You all admired in President Carter?

OBAMA.
Well Joe here's covered that just now I think.
The eulogy was excellent, you had
Us all in tears. I wish I knew him well.
I'm sure there's more I could have learnt

BUSH.
In truth Barack, he was a greater man
Than president. He would have learnt from you.

OBAMA.
Oh George, that's kind.

CHARLIE.
And sir, you knew him well?

CLINTON.
                                    I did, for once
When I was just impeached he called and asked
About young Monica, and how I slept
At night considering her treatment at
My hands. How I'd abused my power, then
Disowned the girl, and left her to the press –
Hey Charlie, this is off the record, right?

HARRIS *enters with* FLOURNOY.

HARRIS.
Permit me all to interrupt. Hey Charlie could we have the room?

CHARLIE.
Of course.

HARRIS.
And Tina, make sure we're not disturbed.

CHARLIE *and* FLOURNOY *go.*

I've heard just now from my security.
Although there was no invitation, Trump,
Arrived regardless, and five minutes late.
In being tardy he did cause a rank
Commotion at the door, which fin'ly was
Resolved by 'llowing him to sit not in
The row with you, but on the balcony.

BUSH.
Thank God for that! I couldn't take his company.

HARRIS.
No not good news, without a doubt this is,
An orchestrated snub, to cultivate
Resentment 'gainst the older guard.
He's here to pay his disrepects –

BIDEN.
                                    But when
It finished, did he leave?

HARRIS.

                    I... I don't –

BIDEN.
Where is he now?

Enter TRUMP.

TRUMP.
A finer question never asked! And one
That's pondered by so many since I was
Unceremoniously evicted by
The eld'ly coven gathered here. Come on!
I'm joking – actually I'm not but still –
Will no one shake my hand? Or smile at least?
Come on!

OBAMA.
            There was no invitation made
To you or any of your hateful crew.
We snub your greeting since we are agreed
You should not have attended here today.

TRUMP.
But he was president, and so was I.

CLINTON.
What sort of man attends a funeral
From which he has specifically been barred?
Perhaps James Carter should have followed in
The playwright Osborne's bitter mourning path
And ordered 'pon the day of burial
A list be nailed onto the chapel door
The names of those who were forbidden from
An entry through to pay respects that day.

TRUMP.
That's actually a good idea, I'll steal
It for myself. Although it wouldn't be
A sheet of paper but a database.
And for your information none of you
Would make that naughty list. You're welcome at
That sad sad day to come and sit just where
You like – cos I'm not proud – yes even if

It's just to check I'm dead. Completely fine.
Except for mad King George. For these were marked
As Democratic enemies from off.
But you were supposed to keep your loyalty
Assured in the very party that
Unlikely as it seemed, did make you and
Your touchy father leaders of the world.

Beat.

But really none of you will shake my hand?
I'm gloved if that makes any difference?

CLINTON.
I have to leave, and so I'm sure, do you?

BUSH.
Yeah right.

OBAMA.
   We'll meet again another day
In private mourning this time, we'll reflect
The sacrifice a man did make to put
His country 'fore himself. I'll see you soon.

OBAMA, BUSH *and* CLINTON *leave*.

TRUMP.
You notice how the air seems fresher now?

HARRIS.
We have to go as well.

TRUMP.
   Is this the way
It works with you these days? The dummy and
His puppet master, helping you to stand,
And pulling strings and speaking proxy words
From out the corner of her mouth.

HARRIS.
     We work
Together sir –

TRUMP.
   That's not what I have heard –

BIDEN.
>   The shame you bring, my president, is twice
>   The shame in that it is so unrequired.
>   I stay polite. I always will, yet you persist:
>   A childish rattle, tantrums, stamping feet.

TRUMP.
>   Okay, well give me then, a chance, and stay.
>   As two decrepit presidents I'd love
>   To chew the fat for just five minutes here.

BIDEN *considers him.*

HARRIS.
>   I'm sorry sir, our schedule makes strict
>   Demands we must proceed apace. We are
>   To visit the late president's family.

TRUMP.
>   And once again I ask the man and here
>   The lady speaks.

BIDEN.
>   Well Kamala is right.

Beat.

>   But yet we have another president's
>   Request. And this one here and now.

HARRIS.
>   I'm sorry sir, we really ought –

BIDEN.
>   You'll have a moment. Kamala perhaps
>   You'll let them know?

HARRIS.
>   ...I... yes, of course.

She makes to go.

TRUMP.
>   And get some orange juice. It's dry in here.

HARRIS *stops for a second, but then goes.*

BIDEN.
You can't resist an insult

TRUMP.
                    No! Not true.
I'm genuinely really thirsty Joe.
And she can tell an aide I'm sure. I'm not
Suggesting that she squeeze the fruit herself.

BIDEN.
Well what shall we discuss? Specific things?
Or simply get to know the other's mind?

TRUMP.
I think we have the measure of our minds.
No my agenda's an agendum here
(That's Latin, which I learned last week, it means
I only have one question.)

BIDEN.
                    Good. Then ask.

TRUMP.
It's simply, are you sure? You want to run?
For even though I'm not the candidate,
I'll with my influence decide the king.
And make damn sure they win.
We'll raid your history. Before the end
We'll tear to shreds a reputation that
You've taken decades building up, and no
Belief in God, nor moral standing can
These days protect you from the Twitterstorm.
Where honour, fact, reality itself
Is question-marked, and melted down, before
Recast as weapons perfectly aligned
To kneecap with a single blow those so
Naive they 'ttempt to stand on higher ground.
Therefore in kindness to an older man
I ask you gently, friend, now are you sure?

BIDEN *smiles*.

BIDEN.

You say it's all about the deal. It's there
In every interaction of your life.
But deals require something underneath.
They stand on *trust*. That's economics Don.
In banks, the markets, government. And if
Those institutions fail, at least the faith
To look a partner in the eye and know
That profit from a year of honest trade
Is worth much more than one day's counterfeit.
Without that trust, there'll be no profit made
No barter, cash, or wealth. The fraud, in time
Finds punishment in exile. Who will deal
With him, the cheat? We all know he lies!
Perhaps that sounds familiar? You think
You'll make the king? Well if that's so
I'm happier than ever to place my trust
In good Americans to cast their vote.
Your question's made me newly galvanised
And here a solid answer: Yes. I'm sure.

TRUMP.

Okay.

HARRIS *enters, with a small glass of orange juice.*

HARRIS.

Apologies for interrupting but
The presidential family awaits.

BIDEN *stands.*

TRUMP.

And now I see just what it is she does.

He reaches out to HARRIS.

HARRIS *sips the orange juice.*

HARRIS.

Oh sorry hon, you want one too?

A moment.

TRUMP.

Before you go –

He removes his gloves.

> Let's do as you suggest
> And make a pact, as men, and shake our hands.
> I offer this respect, my president.
> Whatever happens, won't be personal.

BIDEN *looks.*

HARRIS.
Joe. We need to leave.

BIDEN *thinks. Then takes* TRUMP*'s hand. They shake.*

BIDEN.
Be better. Please.

TRUMP.
> Okay, I'll try, thanks Dad.

TRUMP *suddenly pulls* BIDEN *towards him.*

I know about Jill. What she did?

BIDEN.
What?

TRUMP.
I'll tell everyone.

BIDEN.
Tell them what? There's nothing.

TRUMP.
You sure?

A moment. Then TRUMP *releases him.* BIDEN *looks at him, a little shaken.*

BIDEN.
All this is fantasy. For you are done.
Irrelevant. The king? They wouldn't let
You make the tea. We have to go.

BIDEN *leaves.*

HARRIS *is following, when –*

TRUMP.
  I won't forget the juice. That's rude. So rude.

  She turns back.

HARRIS.
  May I say something?

TRUMP.
                                    It's nice you ask.

HARRIS.
  I see you sir.

TRUMP.
  That's it? Well I see you as well sweetheart.
  I see a lot of things. Great eyes. Such eyes.

HARRIS.
  See what you are.
  In time we will ensure, again, you lose
  I hope you drown in motherfucking juice.

  She makes to go. IVANKA *enters, upstage.*

  Ivanka.

IVANKA.
  Vice-President.

  HARRIS *goes.*

  My father, you're required. For outside
  Supporters of our cause do shout toward
  The Carter family and pelt their car
  With bottles. Yes, our base is loyal but they
  Are still conservative in taste and will
  Not swallow desecration even at
  A democratic figure such as he.

TRUMP.
  A word on politics: If crowds do tend
  Towards your cause, and not commanded by
  Yourself but motivated by their love,
  You'd be a fool if, like a boss who finds
  An interested assistant flirting hard,

You quote a rule and kill the sexy mood.
If I believe in freedom then these guys
Outside have brains, let's leave it up to them.

IVANKA.

You say they're not our doing, and your choice
To come was made last minute. But then on
Arrival how were they already there?
With Trumpish banners primed...?

TRUMP.

What bodes this cross-examination? Does
The scene outside make vomitous your mouth?
Or stomach turn, when missiles thrown, for fear
There might be someone hurt? I thought of all
My brood you shared my lustful course to pick
Desired endpoint then unflinchingly
Proceed. For power never came without the mess.
A victory born of compromise will, as
We know, be shackled to a half-assed win,
So why's my wolf become a shaking chick?

IVANKA.

I'm not a chick but neither am I dumb
And clumsy bull, who smashes things to bits.
What victory? When all we do is give
Our hard-earned clout to someone else's name
The scene outside will bring no power, just
Contempt and general mockery.

TRUMP.

                              Ivanka.
I am concerned. I must be sure your gut's
A furnace, heating flames within that heart
To power thought as sharp as steel.

IVANKA.

My father, be assured, I'm sharp enough.

TRUMP.

Okay. Good.

    TRUMP *exits*.

IVANKA.

    He chooses to compare me to a beast.
    Well I am not his chick or wildest wolf.
    And though I love him still, I grow tired of
    The way he always speaks to me. Therefore
    Perhaps I'll match him for comparison:
    He's not an elephant as many have,
    Or growling stupid rabid dog.
    Why not a smaller beast? He'll be my sheep.
    From here within the trench, where I will stay,
    He'll cross the minefield, and can clear my way.

    IVANKA *exits*.

ACT TWO

2.1

The sound of a Republican rally. The CROWD *raucous –
chanting 'Cruise the Cruz' and 'Ted Ted Ted'.*

CRUZ *appears – a large cheer.*

Watching are IVANKA, ERIC, DON JR., *and then on the other
side,* HEIDI CRUZ, *and* ATTENDANTS.

CRUZ.
Oh what a beautiful morning! In these
Our darkest times, your faces shine like orbs
And give me hope, that we true patriots
Will stand as one with pride and demonstrate
That we don't need to fight like criminals
With metal poles, and guns and baseball bats
Because the greater force is on our side:
The force of justice, righteousness and God.
The more will join us, those of every creed,
Will see that we're not monsters like the rank
Corrupted Media do –

A boo from the CROWD.

                 – do make us out
To be, but occupy the higher ground
Not scared of argument, not shutting down
The platforms meant for all, or cutting off
Most rudely our elected president.
And we would not stand with this strength today
If it were not for that president
Who tried to drain the swamp, who built the wall.
A legend in his time. I'm pleased, so pleased
He's come aboard, as we together make
Our journey
all the way to Washington!

A cheer from the CROWD.

That's right, he loves you too,
And now what's more – he's here today!

Another cheer from the CROWD.

Shall we

Get him to speak?

A huge cheer from the CROWD.

I know! I've missed him too.
Okay well it's a total honour that
He's here to make endorsement for our cause.
Please welcome please, on this historic day
My colleague and I'd say, by now, my friend
The former president of these most high
United States: it's only Donald Trump!

Enter TRUMP. *He shakes hands with* CRUZ, *who stands back.*

TRUMP *goes to the microphone.*

TRUMP.
I've heard it's Biden, once again, that's what
I'm told. Is that what you've all heard as well?
Yeah Sleepy Joe returns. Apparently
He's been the president the last few years.
I didn't notice. All I saw was that
My country, which I love so much, I love
This country, but, you notice this? We fell,
Again, straight to the bottom of the pile
We're laughed at by the Russians, by Iran
And Chinese too, they look at us and think
Correctly, 'Man, they are a joke!' They do.
They screw us every deal. Every time.
Can't understand why we'd want to elect
The living dead as leader, but it makes
Them happy that's for sure. But anyway,
Whatever he's been doing – seems to work.
He's still so popular.

Booing.

I know. I know.
But look, he is. A guy there shouting 'Thief'.
He's got a point. We won that thing, we did.
There is no question about that, for sure.
Would I call it a coup? Conspiracy?
Maybe. There's people call it that a lot.
But Joe, now Joe, he's doing well, so well
I think he just might get another term
I think he really might. I know. I know.
But all's not lost, and that is why I'm here.
Because you all have Ted. Good ol' Ted Cruz!
And Heidi too. You know she's beautiful
Hey Heidi! How are you? Okay these days?
That's good. And here I am to offer my
Endorsement. So what can I tell you 'bout
Our Ted? Well he's an honourable man.
He's honourable in so many ways.
So when he fought me in the primaries
He said some awful things about me, yeah,
'A snivelling coward.' But he doesn't say
It now. Cos Ted's an honourable man.
'A liar pathological', that too,
Until he saw how many votes I got!
So suddenly he's on TV all day
Defending me and saying I'm so great.
Well right, cos Ted's an honourable man.
And yeah, if he's the best we've got, and yeah –
If he's the guy that you all want to run…?

Chanting from the CROWD.

Wait – I can't hear, what's that you're saying there?
Doughnut, you want a doughnut? No. Do not?
Not what? But I've already promised Ted –
No wait that's not the chant, if only it
Was louder still, for then my ageing ears
And even Ted's, might hear what you all crave.
Okay let me repeat the word I hear.
It's… Donald, Donald, Donald, Donald… Duck?

Oh Donald Trump, you mean it's *me* you want?
But no, I'm old, and out of touch, and Ted
He says I've left it much too late to run so...

A cheer from the CROWD.

You think I can? You think I should? But would
I have enough support?

The biggest cheers yet.

                    But what of Ted?

Booing.

Come on, that's not polite, he called you here.
And look I'm working hard at golf right now
I've got no time to be the president
Again. But hey, you know they're pouring in.
I built that wall, but Joe just let them in
To flood across the border, very sad.
And this economy, when I was there?
It was so beautiful, so many jobs.
The unemployment down, the times were good
But now he's giving them away to folks
Who – let's just say their English isn't great.
I might get banned, I might get taken off
TV again! Hey guys, you want to cut
Away right now? You don't? No right, thought not.

More chanting.

Hey – listening to you? You've changed my mind
So here's tomorrow's headline in advance:

'A great surprise! The Donald runs again.'

Okay. I'm in. Are you?

A cheer.

                    And here's a new
Improved and most appealing chant to use
'America Rules. America Rules. America Rules!'

The CROWD *cheer 'America Rules!', as* TRUMP *stands
back.*

We got any ticker tape here?

He looks up and, with a bang, it falls. Music starts.

He turns to CRUZ, *smiles and shrugs.*

Sorry Ted.

With thumbs up, he leaves the stage.

2.2

The campaign party after the rally. Music plays.

CHARLIE *enters, and sees* ROSIE, *who's drinking from a stars-and-stripes paper cup.*

CHARLIE.
    Very patriotic…

    ROSIE *turns and sees him.*

ROSIE.
    Oh! No, what are you – / why are you here

CHARLIE.
    …but not so good for the environment. I'm doing my job, covering the Cruz campaign. But you're working for Ivanka now!

ROSIE.
    Yes I'm / working for Ivanka.

CHARLIE.
    I mean that's… quite a job, isn't it? You've got a hat and everything.

ROSIE.
    You look like Dad when you laugh at people.

CHARLIE.
    You look like Mom when you don't.

A moment.

CHARLIE.
  What's it like?

ROSIE.
  You want a story.

CHARLIE.
  I'm interested.

ROSIE.
  Okay but in me or – no no touching – stand over there, you'll
  infect me with, I don't know –

CHARLIE.
  Compassion?

ROSIE.
  Socialism. You always think I'm – Let me ask *you* a
  question. You're a Democrat and you think you're good
  don't you? You're the good guys.

CHARLIE.
  Yeah I think the Democratic Party is on the side of causes
  that I believe in like equality of opportunity. Fairness, /
  kindness, maybe, human rights –

ROSIE.
  Okay so yes, and that's interesting because we don't. We don't
  see ourselves as good and you as bad. We see ourselves as
  realists. And see you as naive. Weak. / Desperate and corrupt.

CHARLIE.
  You really think I'm weak?

ROSIE.
  You ever fired a gun?

CHARLIE.
  I don't approve of / guns.

ROSIE.
  I've never seen you work out.

CHARLIE.
  Sometimes –

ROSIE.
You do martial arts?

CHARLIE.
Does yoga count?

ROSIE.
You got kids yet?

CHARLIE.
Since we last spoke six months ago? / No.

ROSIE.
But would you kill a stranger if they were going to hurt them?

CHARLIE.
If I had kids?

ROSIE.
If you had kids would you kill a stranger who was about to / hurt them?

CHARLIE.
Yeah.

ROSIE.
No.

CHARLIE.
I would.

ROSIE.
You would not. You would try to kill them. But they would overpower you because you hadn't worked out in the gym. Because you don't own or know how to fire a gun. Because all you've got is *yoga*. You talk about white privilege, you write about that a lot, well it's the greatest privilege to believe that when it comes to it, someone else is going to protect you. That there's someone, in your police force, in Washington that genuinely gives a crap. They don't. So what I believe, what *we* believe, is recognising that and giving each person as much individual freedom as possible. That's what Trump understands.

CHARLIE.
You've really thought it through.

ROSIE.
Charlie, I'm *Ivanka's fucking driver / of course I've* –

CHARLIE.
Yes you / are.

ROSIE.
Jesus, you're still *sneering* –

CHARLIE.
I just want to understand.

ROSIE.
You can't.

CHARLIE.
No come on I mean how does it work? The supporters? You
have meetings or what? Turn up with flags, guns whatever,
make your plans, listen to important people –

ROSIE.
Yeah.

CHARLIE.
I mean it won't be like that but –

ROSIE.
It is. It's exactly like that. One next Thursday.

CHARLIE.
Oh. Okay. So can I come?

ROSIE *laughs*.

ROSIE.
No! They would tear you to pieces. You're not just a
Democrat but a *reporter*. I mean, they would literally take
one look and –

CHARLIE.
How would they know?

ROSIE.
The way you talk, your hair –

CHARLIE.
What's the problem with my hair?

ROSIE.
You ever think there's a whole world / you don't know anything about.

CHARLIE.
Rosie, we used to be close. We used to laugh.

ROSIE.
You laughed.

Beat.

CHARLIE.
Okay okay yes you're right, okay, you don't make sense to me, at all. How someone educated and... good... could want to support... *him*.

ROSIE.
Let's just stop this / conversation.

CHARLIE.
So *show* me. Please. At least we'll spend some time together... That would be good right?

I miss Mom and Dad too.

TRUMP *enters with* IVANKA, *and sees them.*

TRUMP.
Who's the guy Rosie? Doesn't look your type.

ROSIE.
He – oh my God, he's not – he's going.

CHARLIE.
Call me.

ROSIE.
Okay.

CHARLIE *turns and goes.* ROSIE *turns to* TRUMP *and smiles.*

Congratulations sir.

TRUMP *turns to* IVANKA.

TRUMP.
Have you seen all the happy faces here?

IVANKA.
I wish you'd made me prior confidante.

TRUMP.
Does God give proof, or warning of his plans?
Course not. For then you'd have no need for faith.

ERIC *enters*.

ERIC.
      Hey Dad! So cool!
When stepping out today, you'd no idea
That you would finally run? It truly was
The lively crowd that changed your wav'ring mind?

TRUMP.
Er yeah. That's right. They wanted it and I
Would be the rudest guy to not oblige.

(*Aside to* IVANKA.) If Eric is so swift convinced I think
We can assume the story's landed well.

Enter CRUZ *and* HEIDI.

CRUZ.
You cannot be a man. For even the
Most base and vile excuse for human being
Would hesitate to lie like you, to cheat

TRUMP.
Hey careful Ted, don't make a twice mistake
Into a hat trick. Maybe there's a place
For you inside my tightest hellish ring.
Depends. You've horns but can you wear the tail?
If so then come, let's talk like adult men.

Beat.

CRUZ.
Of course, it's true, we both have our support.
If there were –

HEIDI *steps forward and slaps* TRUMP. SECURITY *steps forward.* TRUMP *holds them back.*

HEIDI.

If he accepts so much as typist to
Your rank and fascist cause he will I swear
Be typing as my former husband and
No father to our children. You know not
What we have been through. You have no idea
What suffering is. Your life's been charmed.
I hope one day you face a torturer
Who measures unto you the pain that you
Have sunk into the wealth of humankind.

TRUMP.

You see? I always said that if you'd not
The craziness you were near thrice the man
You married. Take your pills and hide the tears
(And maybe change the hair), then stand instead
Of me, and Heidi, you would get my vote.

HEIDI.

I promise I'll not rest until the day
When all can happ'ly stand or crouching piss
Upon your unmarked, pauper's lowly grave.
For I have had a dream: You'll die alone.

TRUMP.

Alone?

A moment, then HEIDI *turns and goes.* CRUZ *looks at* TRUMP.

If she is seeing a professional,
I'd get your money back. For here's the truth:
If not for her you'd be vice-president.

CRUZ *turns and goes.*

DON JR.

But Father there's a crowd of congressmen
And senators, next door, who having paid
Allegiance to the Cruz, stand outraged at
Your swift usurping of his cause, they say
They want to speak with you immediately.

TRUMP.
  Then send them in.

DON JR.

                  Okay.

TRUMP.

                  And you'll explain.

IVANKA.
  I will?

TRUMP.
            That's right. For unlike Pence, or Biden,
            I do assume that if you get the job
            You'll not be just a silent partner right?

IVANKA.
  Oh God, you mean...

TRUMP.

                  You show me what you'll do.

IVANKA.
  I'm thankful Dad. Your faith will be repaid!

  She goes.

DON JR.
  Like Pence and Biden? You mean...

TRUMP.
  Oh Don, why don't you have a special think?

  He does, as a party of CONGRESSMEN *and* SENATORS
  enter, with IVANKA.

IVANKA.
  For those of you who've never met him here's
  The President of the United States,
  Which is what all will call him now, not just
  Emeritus, but also what he is
  This moment, if they'd counted all the votes.

  The OHIO SENATOR *steps forward.*

OHIO.
My president. You long had my support
In office, but we stand, I'd say, upset.
The race was had.
With one debate to go,
All rivals now withdrawn to give
Ted Cruz the clearest route to victory.
We've put our best resource behind his cause,
And understood you were attending here
Today to do the same.

IVANKA.
But congressman,
You did just hear the crowd?

OHIO.
I did indeed.

IVANKA.
Then surely you cannot ignore their call.
Their *preference*. Unless you want to lose?

OHIO *looks unsure. Then turns back to* TRUMP.

OHIO.
We want to understand precisely what
Our president does now intend.

IVANKA.
Okay.
Okay, well here's the plan. It's very clear.
Once heard, you'll have a choice. You're in. Or out.
The president will run again and win.
And standing as his running mate will be
A loyal, diverse, and energetic choice
In fact I was his instinct years ago.

OHIO.
You mean yourself?

IVANKA.
Indeed, well done.
My father brings his base but I will reach
A generation new, more urban, young,

But sick of paying tax and service to
A stifling culture they do not believe.
They crave the freedom of their fathers, who
Would go with pride to work, not shamed by their
Ambition, gender, colour of their skin,
But proud! Your father sir, now was he proud?

OHIO.

Proud of his country madam, yes he was.

IVANKA.

I bet he was. For it's America! There was
A buck to make, and make with joy not fear,
Our fathers built our cities, markets and
Ensured as superpower we did rule.
We *ruled* not served. Did not apologise
For power, grovelling guilty at the feet
Of lesser men, or feel the constant need
To justify ourselves. We did, not talked.
We built a glorious empire, and as we built.
The world did not complain, but happ'ly bought.
And as they bought, the poor got richer right
Around the globe. All this we will restore.
But here I warn you all:
The president this time won't countenance
Dissent from party or establishment.
We know he has the people's willing vote.
The fight's instead to ratify their choice.
So you now face a choice yourselves.
You stay before us, telling us you're in.
You pledge support, in turn your vic'try waits.
Or leave the room, and fail in all you do.

A moment.

The group remains.

TRUMP.

Well there you are. You look at that. All in.
I'll tell you now, instead of picking your
Vice-president from off the same old tree,
You plant a little seed, and having sown,
Before you know it, look: You've grown your own!

He lifts his glass.

Ivanka!

They toast her. He hugs her. Photos, drinking, celebration.

A party.

ACT THREE

3.1

The White House mess. Night. A storm rages outside.

HARRIS *enters, looking for biscuits.*

HARRIS.
    An understudy is poor consolation.
    You have to be there every night, and know
    The lines. Aware you'd do as well as he
    That struts and frets each night upon the stage
    Though chances are you'll not be called upon.
    Instead your skills remain unseen, within
    The lonely dressing room. So why did I
    Accept this shadow role? A quiet vice
    To the elected chief? Because I knew
    The country needed a decisive win.
    My own career meant naught compared to that.
    But since that day, despite attempts to forge
    A strong connection, I am left alone.
    Cut from the busy president. And now,
    With news of Trump's return, they all seem sure
    That our pragmatic choice should stay. Our man
    From yesterday to bring tomorrow's joy.
    And this I get. I made the case myself.
    And yet, at night, my mind it listless strays.
    Was it a misplaced modesty perhaps
    That made me push old Joe to run once more?
    Should I instead have seized the worn baton
    From off the tired cove, who nobly had
    Already trod his marathon and run
    The long-desired race myself? For if
    The house is burning, staying still means death.

    Obama was made president because
    He was a triple threat; he never hid

His blackness or his maleness, but equally
He never made them reason for your vote.
Instead the third persuasion was the best.
The way his speech, and deeds and rhetoric
Inspired feeling. Faith. And 'yes we can'.
That's what I hoped. To run as female, black,
With pride, and with my head aloft, but with
The ballots cast on me and what I'll do.
I'm sure I'm more than deputy. Much more
Than prosecuting ace. Well sure I was...
Since if one runs for president you must
Believe you're not just representing, but
Unique. That from a populous that counts
Three hundred million souls, you are the one.
But maybe ego's not my natural state.
A best supporting actor, not the lead.

Enter FLOURNOY.

FLOURNOY.

    Just now, when up at work, I hear a crash,
    I think it must be spectral force, that I
    Should call the Ghostbusters (by which I mean
    The one with Kristen Wiig and Leslie Jones)

HARRIS.

    Me too I love that film.

FLOURNOY.

                Instead I go,
    And there discover not a ghoul but our
    Vice-President of these United States
    Who wanders, hopeless, looking for the tin
    Of cookies her considerate and quite
    Good-looking chief-of-staff did contribute
    A single day before. A sorry sight.

HARRIS.

    This is the last?

FLOURNOY.

              Well sure.

HARRIS.

I couldn't sleep.

FLOURNOY.
I guessed. But why?

HARRIS.

I heard the crash myself.

FLOURNOY.
Then if not you then what did make the noise?

HARRIS.
Did I do wrong?

FLOURNOY.

You mean?

HARRIS.

Persuading Joe

To run again?

Beat.

FLOURNOY.
You want the truth?

HARRIS.

That's what the nights are for.

Beat.

FLOURNOY.
I always felt you had capacity
For greater fate than vice to anyone.

HARRIS.
So then, did I do *wrong*?

FLOURNOY.

You long considered.
If wrong or right, that judgement comes with time.

HARRIS.
By which point it's too late. I want it now!
From you! Unvarnished and most blunt.

FLOURNOY.
> Then yes. You did. Vice-President.
> I think you got it wrong.

HARRIS.

>   Okay.

HARRIS opens the cookie tin. There's none left.

> Well it's irrelevant. The question speaks
> More of my ego than what's genuinely best
> We've chosen: Joe will stand again, and I
> Vice-president again and done is done.

Another crash, from off to the right.

They both look over.

> We should call security.

Enter RICHETTI, bedraggled.

> Hey Steve, it's late for even you. But... God
> You look so pale.

RICHETTI.

>   The president's awake.

HARRIS.

>   Right now?

RICHETTI.
> Indeed. He's on his way

HARRIS.

>   Hey Steve.
> What's going on?

RICHETTI.

>   I can't –

Enter BIDEN. He staggers, distracted, still asleep, but walking.

> This is the first you've stayed within the house
> In months, but for the last few weeks he has
> Most every night been walking, yet asleep.

And seemed distracted and quite… ill.
I follow, making sure no harm does come.

FLOURNOY.
For weeks?

RICHETTI.
Yes ever since the day on which
The former president was laid to rest.

BIDEN *looks off in another direction suddenly.*

But 'tis most… worrying. The things he says!

HARRIS.
He speaks?

RICHETTI.
Oh yes. Most uninhibited.
Another cause for my attendance. To
Ensure the words will not be heard.

HARRIS.
Uh – Joe?

RICHETTI.
Disturb him not, I beg of you!
He'll only get upset.

BIDEN.
It's late to change too late I know

HARRIS.
Change what?

BIDEN.
But change I must. I must. For what we do
Is meaningless without a certainty
Within our hearts. And Jill. It's wrong
We're so old, us both –

HARRIS.
Joe at the funeral what did he say?

BIDEN.
The funeral?

HARRIS.

> Yes! Trump. He seized you by
> The hand and whispered roughly in your ear

BIDEN.

> He has no conscience. Please! Don't make me run!
> But yes I must. For if I don't he'll win again.
> I need Jill, the kids, I need my *life*, what's left
> For it's so late, they've given up so much.

He calms down as HARRIS *helps* BIDEN *into a chair.*

HARRIS.

> You said it started after the service

RICHETTI.

> That's right. For there were many greeted at
> The funeral, and as we've come to know
> Too well, a small disease can spread unbound.

HARRIS.

> But it was cold that day and when he shook
> The hands of those in church, each one of them,
> Including him were all still wearing gloves.

FLOURNOY.

> Then from a hug perhaps, or something else?

HARRIS.

> He only took them off while waiting with
> The other presidents, and having met
> Already, none of them shook hands again

RICHETTI.

> So what's your point?

HARRIS.

> 'Twas very strange that Trump
> Arrived like that, so uninvited when
> So much abhorred. He usually stays away.

FLOURNOY.

> You're saying –

HARRIS.

                   – saying Joe shook hands with just
A single person without gloves that day
And at the former president's behest.

RICHETTI.

You think he… poisoned him?!

HARRIS.

I don't know.

RICHETTI.

Madam Vice-President I've known not what
To do. For every night he circles round
That only he can win the vote against
The former president but yet can't face
The baying circus and the scrutiny
Tomorrow is the first of the debates
But he cannot attend like this.

BIDEN.

Kamala.

    HARRIS *stands and goes to him.*

BIDEN.

        My thoughts
Don't stay for long, my words are…
It hasn't worked. I came with such great dreams
To end the carnage. Unite us all
Again. To get more done! But party lines
Have grown to walls that no one passes through
I tried to bring the sides together but
Their phones and apps do by design enrage
And carve them up. All limits on the lies,
The personal attacks, all honour's… gone.
I may be thought the safest pair of hands.
But safety never won a war.

HARRIS.

                         It's not
A war.

BIDEN.

It feels that way. I'm hurt by age
And disappointment.
I cannot fight again.
He has no conscience. What he'll do. But please.
Don't make me run! There'll be polite
Objection but you'll get no more than that.
And it's your obligation right, your pledge?
You'll be sworn in tonight.

HARRIS.

You'll… swear me in? You want me candidate?
Okay, but we don't –

BIDEN.

– I can't. I won't go on.
We'll use the twenty-fifth

HARRIS.

You mean
Use section three, a temporary pass
Of office on to me, until you are –

BIDEN.

No, section one. I need to speak to Jill,
The kids, I need my *life* again – what's left –
I will resign tonight, you will accede, which means
That with the twenty-fifth you will be made
The forty-seventh. My friend you are
A woman with capacity that in truth
I never had.

HARRIS.

There's not a person here, or in your staff,
Who would agree to this –

BIDEN.

There's not a person here who would refuse.
(*To* RICHETTI.) Bible.

RICHETTI *hesitates, then goes.*

HARRIS.

Joe, you're ill –

BIDEN.

I've given all I have
In service of the state but now...
And this is what you wanted, no? You ran against me
For president, back then you seemed so sure –
What's happened now?

RICHETTI *re-enters with an* OFFICIAL *holding the Bible,
and with other witnesses and staff.*

Just place your hand upon the Bible here.
Just place your hand.
I tapped you as vice-president because
I saw a rare integrity,
And you said yes because you felt it too.

He looks at her.

Was I wrong?

Please...

He goes down on his knees.

Please Kamala...

She looks at him. Around at the others. A moment.

Then she walks to him and puts out her hand.

HARRIS.

My president, there is no need to beg.
We have your orders and
We will obey.
With three lifetimes of service, you have earned
The right to rest.

He takes her hand and stands.

BIDEN.

Kamala. My thanks.

A moment. BIDEN *sits. Rests.*

HARRIS.

(*To* FLOURNOY.) I'll need more cookies after this.

FLOURNOY.
> They say that when we make our plans the gods
> Do laugh. But in this case I wonder if
> They have not interfered but made amends.

> *HARRIS turns to* RICHETTI.

RICHETTI.
> Shall we proceed?

> *A moment. Then* HARRIS *nods.*

> Madam Vice-President, repeat after me:
> I do solemnly swear

> *HARRIS turns and talks to us as* RICHETTI *keeps speaking.*

> that I will faithfully execute the Office of President of the
> United States –

HARRIS.
> My fellow Americans
> Tonight our president, Joe Biden, has
> Been taken ill. We're giving him the best
> Of care, repayment for the years he's served.
> But Joe's decided in the interest of
> A stable government, and mindful that
> The national elections do approach,
> He would withdraw as candidate this time
> And furthermore resign from office. So
> About two hours hence, I did fulfill
> My oath and duly was sworn in as
> The forty-seventh president of these
> United States.

> We're founded on a dream, made real, that all
> Are welcome here to live, to thrive, to give
> To all an equal opportunity.
> And that's what I will promise you, that if
> You're Black, Latino, Native American
> South Asian, white, wherever you come from
> This is still your United States.
> I will not let you down. For God bless you.
> And God bless our wonderful country too.

3.2.

A bar. Music plays. There's a small stage. TRUMP
SUPPORTERS *mill around. They are dressed in varying levels
of costume – some in normal clothes, others dressed in strange
costumes (like the QAnon Shaman).*

*The make-up of the others needs to exactly reflect the national
demographic make-up of Trump's supporter base.*

ROSIE *enters with* CHARLIE. CHARLIE's *dressed in a
checkered shirt, badly fitting jeans, and glasses.*

ROSIE.
    What is this? Seattle 1993?

CHARLIE.
    Yeah / okay.

ROSIE.
    We're Trump supporters not the fucking Pearl Jam fan club.

CHARLIE.
    You've dressed down.

ROSIE.
    What? Yeah I'm not going to come in my uniform / if
    that's –

CHARLIE.
    No but you used to dress well, smart. Not any more. This is a
    uniform too, in a way. You want to fit in.

ROSIE.
    Maybe I do. These are good people Charlie.

CHARLIE.
    Not all / of them.

ROSIE.
    Not all of them but a lot of them. They never judge me.
    They're hard-working people who feel like they're always
    being laughed at, and lied to, and are you really sure they're
    not? I've read some of your pieces.

CHARLIE.
    I just write down what they say. If that sounds funny to you –

ROSIE.
    There you go. That's the tone.

CHARLIE.
    What do you mean?

ROSIE.
    You look down on them. Jesus, if we're going to do this
    you've gotta be at least a little honest. You *know* what I / mean

CHARLIE.
    Alright. I know what you mean but it's that or giving these
    people a free pass to say whatever offensive things they want
    just because they feel left behind, because they're *good in
    their heart*.

ROSIE.
    No but –

CHARLIE.
    And that's patronising. I say it like I see it.

ROSIE.
    Yeah so do I.

CHARLIE.
    Because the truth is important.

ROSIE.
    The truth is everything.

CHARLIE.
    Okay. Well, maybe we're not so different then.

    PAUL *enters and heads to the stage.*

ROSIE.
    Just stay next to me and shut up. Okay? Not a word?

CHARLIE.
    Okay.

ROSIE.
    I need a 'yes Rosie I'll keep my fucking mouth / closed
    throughout'

CHARLIE.
    Yes Rosie I'll keep my fucking mouth / closed throughout.

PAUL takes to the stage with a microphone.

PAUL.
    How we feeling?! You ready?

CROWD.
    Yeah!

PAUL.
    Okay! Two hours till the debate and while we wait, we've
    got some incredible people. The woman who started it all –
    Tracy Beans.

A cheer.

    And the whistle-blower, the truth-teller – former National
    Security Advisor to Donald Trump, General Michael Flynn!

A huge cheer.

    And then it's our guy versus Ka*m*ala, the unelected
    president –

CHARLIE.
    Kamala.

PAUL.
    What?

CHARLIE.
    No – hey – sorry – I just think it's pronounced Kamala?

PAUL.
    That's – okay – we'll talk about *Kamala* in a second but
    before we do I've been told that we have an intruder in our
    midst. A reporter.

A reaction. PAUL starts to walk amongst the CROWD.

    Well obviously it's a new face…

He walks closer and closer to CHARLIE.

    But I know. I have their *identity*. Their photograph… And
    here… they… are.

He suddenly turns away from CHARLIE *to a man on the front row.*

Right?

MATT *stands. A big reaction from the* CROWD.

MATT.
Yes alright. Matt Bodey, from the BBC – I'm making a podcast about the Trump campaign, we actually / tried to approach you –

PAUL.
This is a private meeting.

MATT.
We want to understand / how you work, your ideas –

PAUL.
Mainstream media everyone!

Someone puts their hands on MATT.

MATT.
The level of violence in your organisation.

PAUL.
The level of violence.

PAUL *reaches out and grabs* MATT*'s Dictaphone, puts it under his foot and breaks it, as* MATT *is roughly escorted out.*

That clear to you?!

So, now it's just *us*, when the debate starts, we've work to do. The first test of our freedom. Strength by any means. We've got instructions – come prepared.

CHARLIE*'s got his hand up.* ROSIE*'s fighting with him to put it down.*

Yes friend?

ROSIE.
No, no, it's nothing, / ignore him –

CHARLIE.
What does that mean? 'Come prepared.'

PAUL.
Who are you?

CHARLIE.
I'm… Charles.

PAUL.
Charles, being prepared in this country is whatever you need to feel like you can defend yourself, you family, your way of life.

CHARLIE.
Sounds… dangerous.

PAUL.
Who brought you Charles?

ROSIE.
Er… I did. He's a friend with a big mouth.

PAUL.
Tell your friend the risk we face is nothing compared to the danger of leaving our country in the hands of the rich and corrupted few, who steal our choices, our businesses, our freedom of speech. We're doing what folks have always done. Ensuring our voice is heard. So, tonight be ready! And when he gives you the word, show your love. Your love for country –

A cheer

For freedom!

Another cheer.

And for Donald fucking Trump!

A big cheer. 'American Rules!'

Tracey Beans is on her way. Five minutes.

Music starts again. People stand – go their separate ways.

ROSIE.
Okay you made a promise, I'm taking this seriously. / They said they'd –

CHARLIE.
I'm taking this seriously.

ROSIE.
I do all this, I get you in, as a favour, because I think maybe you can just keep your mouth shut and do what I say –

CHARLIE.
It's just me finding out about it –

ROSIE.
No you were accusing, judging, this is *important* to me, it really is, so go away, go away now. I'm getting a drink.

She walks off to get a drink. CHARLIE*'s about to head towards the door when* PAUL *approaches with some other large guys.*

PAUL.
Charles.

He turns.

You got a lot of questions. Come on. Let's talk.

CHARLIE *looks at them, unsure.*

CHARLIE.
Okay.

He goes with them, taking his bag. ROSIE *comes back.*

ROSIE.
Okay. Charlie, we'll give it one more go –

She looks around. He's gone. But his coat is still on the chair...

Charlie?

She heads off, looking for him.

3.3

Pre-debate.

TRUMP, IVANKA, *and* ATTENDANTS *enter.*

TRUMP.
 The cars?

IVANKA.
                    Will all be waiting parked outside.

TRUMP.
 The dinner wasn't good, what we just had.

IVANKA.
 I know.

TRUMP.
                 You get ahold the boss you say
 That Donald came and tried to eat his food
 But was so underwhelmed, you say he missed
 An opportunity so big, so big.

HARRIS *enters separately, opposite, with* FLOURNOY,
RICHETTI, *her* SPEECHWRITER, ATTENDANTS, *and*
SECURITY.

RICHETTI.
 Just never patronise the man, you'll seem –

HARRIS.
 Like Hillary I know, it doesn't wash

FLOURNOY.
 But equally don't let him dominate –

RICHETTI.
 If stating facts, make sure you keep them short.

HARRIS.
 Okay, okay.

FLOURNOY.
 Madam President?

HARRIS.

Yes?

FLOURNOY.

You take a breath.

TRUMP *and* HARRIS *calmly go to their podiums. The*
MODERATOR *enters.*

MODERATOR.

It's an historic night. We're good to go?

HARRIS.

I am.

TRUMP.

Oh yeah. Let's light this country up.

Lights on suddenly.

MODERATOR.

So welcome to the University
Of Michigan and this, our first debate.
And on my right the former president.
It's Donald Trump. Opposing him we have
Here on my left our current president,
Kamala Harris. So:
The format's been agreed by teams of both
Our candidates, I'll pose a question, then
You have two minutes for an answer, and
Your rival can respond. Once done you'll have
Another minute for a free debate.

TRUMP.

But just to say, I'm very happy if
We bench the rules and work a little more
Ad hoc?

MODERATOR.

I'm sorry sir? We've all agreed.

TRUMP.

Hey Kamala, come on! What do you say?

HARRIS.

You know, if it was anybody else?
I would be very happy to agree.

But you're the king of interruption so
Perhaps let's stay with / what we –

TRUMP.

Fine you're scared, okay.

HARRIS.
Not scared at all, just keen that they can hear.

MODERATOR.
And now we're running late before I've asked
A single question.

TRUMP.

Maybe you should have spent
Less time explaining, anyone with sense
Has switched us off by now and got straight back
To season eight of *Selling Sunset* God
I love that show –

MODERATOR.

So our first question is
For President Harris –

TRUMP.

Yeah I've got one
You know the day they stormed the Capitol?
Who was that guy?

MODERATOR.

Sir please adhere / to the –

TRUMP.
He led them up the hill, he broke the fence
He's at the lead, you see him on the day

HARRIS.
Slow down, what guy?

TRUMP.

You don't know 'bout this?
Well we all do – Ray Epps! He's called Ray Epps.
He's on the FBI Most Wanted list
But then when they arrested all the guys
Who did it, hauled them in / and locked them up

MODERATOR.

    No President for / this debate you will commit
    To strictly stay within the rules you have agreed.

TRUMP.

    He's nowhere to be seen! And here's what's more
    Ray's suddenly come off their wanted list!
    They closed their ranks, and said he did no wrong
    And when they're asked if he was one of them,
    An agent there inciting / violence worse
    Than anyone they simply say –

HARRIS.

                  Okay

I know / what you're –

TRUMP.

             They cannot comment.

MODERATOR.

                      President /

If you desire this debate to carry on –

HARRIS.

    So everyone should note that when Donald
    Begins to feels he's losing he will shout
    'Conspiracy'

TRUMP.

          It's facts, you look it up.
    So Kamala, we're talking now, you want
    To ask me something in reply?

HARRIS.

    Perhaps for those all watching we should stick
    More closely to the format, otherwise
    We'll simply get more Donald mouthing off –

TRUMP.

    Well they'd be fine with that, they really would
    And lots of them, they like you too, but who's
    This woman here? I don't know who she is?
    There's all these podcasters, and YouTubers
    They get so many hundred millions
    We should have gone with one of them.

Cos no offence, at least they've got something
To say.

MODERATOR.
> They may indeed, but I am not
> The voice they wish to hear instead it's you
> They want to / listen

TRUMP.
> Right! To us, so stop.
> And by the way for those at home, if you
> Get bored by this and wish instead to go
> Outside and have a party, show your love
> For freedom and our great great country, well,
> That surely would be beautiful, so good.

HARRIS.
Okay I have a question.

TRUMP.
> Sure.

HARRIS.
> After
> Four years and many millions put in.
> What evidence have all your people found
> To offer proof of electoral fraud?

TRUMP.
We've evidence. A lot of evidence

HARRIS.
That's great. So can we see it then?

TRUMP.
> You... Sure.

HARRIS.
You'll put it on your website / then, so we –

TRUMP.
I've got another one for you.

HARRIS.
> Okay
The subject's changed.

MODERATOR.

/ If Madam President –

TRUMP.

You've been in / office now three years

HARRIS.

/ It's fine.

TRUMP.

And what have you achieved? I mean there's lots
Got worse. Much worse. Afghanistan, Ukraine
The Covid laws, that killed our businesses, /
There's nothing passed that I can see except
Environmental trash –

HARRIS.

Rejoined the climate deal, engaged Iran,
We saved more hundreds from a Covid death,
And made / provision to ensure –

TRUMP.

You see all the rehearsal there?

HARRIS.

/ Excuse me sir I'm speaking

TRUMP.

She's talking from a page, not with the heart.

HARRIS.

…I'm speaking.

And for the record I'm speaking from reality.

A small bang from outside.

TRUMP.

You've undone stuff I did, but what of yours?
Cos I look at your friend Obama's time,
The long eight years he had and ask just what
Exactly he achieved? –

HARRIS.

He'd have done more
If not for your obstructive colleagues

TRUMP.

Oh

What a surprise it's all my fault again.

HARRIS.

Your faults are many yes, so why don't we
Revert the question back on you? Despite
Your claims to make us great, you left us with
A state of sorry disarray.
With China stronger, nothing done in North
Korea, and Covid deaths all soaring high. So what
Besides corrupted pardons, and some golf,
Did you achieve?

TRUMP.

So many things.

HARRIS.

Let's start with one.

A moment. TRUMP *caught out for a second.*

Then a louder bang. The MODERATOR *gets a message.*

MODERATOR.

If you can hear a noise,
Apparently it's people in the street
Outside who've got some fireworks, they are
I'm told being escorted far away.

TRUMP.

Wait, why?

There's nothing wrong with fireworks! Perhaps
They're simply having fun?

He turns to camera.

Don't let them tell you what to do, okay?

Another noise – and CROWD *sounds growing.*

HARRIS.

I think the country will be pleased to hear
I let the experts make assessments / as
To the security and safety of
The people both inside and in the street.

TRUMP.
>She stands as leader yet forever lets
>Her 'experts' make the calls, perhaps in case
>She gets it wrong, there's always someone else
>To blame.

FLOURNOY comes onto the stage, and speaks to HARRIS, gives her a piece of paper.

>   Oh look, well here's one now, I thought
>We're having a debate, to help these folks
>To choose their next president,
>But something else is more important, fine.

HARRIS turns back to the stand.

HARRIS.
>Excuse me for a second, President
>And moderator, I've just been told
>Of happenings across the country, all
>With flames, or pyrotechnics, some with masks,
>If peaceful then it's fine, but here I need
>To say if there's a breach of law tonight
>I will enforce it firmly.

TRUMP.
>   People want
>To show their love and in a moment you,
>Like princes to a frog, do turn them all
>To criminals. But these are average guys
>And girls, good people probably –

From inside a shout.

CROWD.
>Donald Trump! Donald Trump!

TRUMP.
>Oh look there's one in here.

He's taken away by SECURITY.

>   Hey let him speak!
>If we're allowed this platform why should he
>Be violently denied the same.

HARRIS.

This is an orchestration, not
Grassroots but organised confusion, all –

TRUMP.

Well that's a claim. I hope you have the proof?
Cos I'm well known for devastating suits.

HARRIS.

I'm sure I'll find some proof, and when I do
I promise I won't keep it to myself –

More stand up in the CROWD *and start chanting. 'America Rules!'*

TRUMP.

Well look at that. He got it right.
You know…

TRUMP *takes off his microphone.*

I think we're missing all the fun.

HARRIS.

You walking away now?

SECURITY *comes up to* HARRIS, *keen to take her away.*

MODERATOR.

But President –

HARRIS.

Donald, you want to finish this?

He stops and looks at her for a moment.

TRUMP.

Oh Kamala, I want it finished so much.
With love, and style. That's why I'm going out
To see myself the passion. You should come.
(*To the cameras.*) All of you!
Enjoy the flames of freedom, brook no bar
To what the constitution guaranteed.
And why not film yourself? And TikTok too
And broadcast to the world the night that we
Reclaimed our country. Come on!

HARRIS.
I'll never play by your rules

TRUMP.
Oh Kamala. These days?

There are no rules.

Flanked by SECURITY, TRUMP *walks off the stage, as the* CROWD *surrounds him. He walks through the auditorium, into the bar.*

America Rules! America Rules!

From now, the world outside – the carnivalesque pageant – starts to intrude on the debate. Fireworks, costumes, cheering and a smell of danger. We also hear the sound of a helicopter growing louder –

The worlds collapse into each other:

IVANKA *watching and applauding.*

CHARLIE *on the street, being taken through the streets by the* CROWD *from the meeting.*

HARRIS, *on the roof, windswept by Marine One above, looking down on the carnage below.*

Chanting outside, in the auditorium, everywhere.

CROWD.
America Rules! America Rules! America Rules!

Sudden blackout.

Interval.

ACT FOUR

4.1.

Night.

As the audience re-enters from the interval, the stage is a chaotic and absurd street party. Flaming torches. Costumes. Confederate flags. Music.

It seems jubilant and, although enthusiastic, not violent or threatening.

After clearance is given, a group of men, including PAUL, *walk on with* CHARLIE.

One of the most strangely dressed figures goes up to them, as the music plays.

Suddenly the music stops. A cheer.

PAUL.
    Scared?
    Don't be scared.
    We're celebrating.

    A cheer.

CHARLIE.
    Okay. Okay. Can I go then? I want to go.

PAUL.
    You want to go?

CHARLIE.
    Yeah, back to my partner. My job. My apartment.

PAUL.
    Your partner. Okay. Your *partner.* You want to go? Sure.

    CHARLIE *turns to go, but one of them blocks his way.*

CHARLIE.
Okay.

PAUL.
Just tell us the truth.

CHARLIE.
What?

PAUL.
About crooked Hillary. And her murdering husband.

CHARLIE.
Look –

PAUL.
How you fixed the election. What really happened at the
Capitol that day. The vaccine.

Cos we're all talking about all of that all the time, but from
you, from all of *you*? Nothing.

He gets out his phone and starts filming.

We're going to fix the mainstream media, right here.

Tell the truth. On camera. And you can go.

CHARLIE.
The truth is what I do for a living. I check / sources,
evidence

PAUL.
You want to protect your *friends*. You deal in lies, so much
you never say – off the record, behind closed doors, making
deals on stories. You shut things down. Well not today.

Say it now.

Crooked Hillary.
Her murdering husband.
Stolen election.
The Capitol.
The vaccine.

CHARLIE.
Or what?

PAUL.
   Or we'll change the way you see things.

   A moment.

CHARLIE.
   No.

   They grab him and pull him offstage, as…

   ROSIE *appears, looking for him… But he's gone.*

4.2

HARRIS *enters and the next scene begins immediately in the Situation Room. Following* HARRIS *are* FLOURNOY, RICHETTI, GENERAL TAYLOR *(Chief of the Armed Forces)*, HEAD OF THE FBI, HEAD OF THE CIA *and other* ATTENDANTS.

HARRIS.
   Fatalities?

RICHETTI.
            So far in tens but it's hard
   To get the information that we need

TAYLOR.
   I'm certain it will be in hundreds, or
   Perhaps far more than that, if we cannot
   In haste extinguish that which fuels the flames.

HARRIS.
   He still encourages the action now?

FLOURNOY.
   His right hand gestures peace while yet his left
   Does wave them on. He found, born from the day
   The Capitol was stormed, a formula
   Enabling violence through a mob that he
   Did knowingly raise and then at once disown

TAYLOR.
We need a curfew.

HARRIS.
But we do not have
Authority to make a law like that

FLOURNOY.
The states will take some time to challenge it
So that's a problem for the future you.
But crucially, so long as you have the
Support of each and every agency –

FBI.
Which here you do.

CIA.
And here.

TAYLOR.
And here as well.
A curfew's blunt but most will understand

HARRIS.
It would confirm what all these marches cry
That in pursuit of larger government
We trash our freedom for authority.

FLOURNOY.
But Kamala if we don't, then more will die.
And there's a further measure we propose…

HARRIS.
As if that's not enough –

RICHETTI.
To stem the tide
We must arrest the former president.

HARRIS.
You…

Beat. She smiles.

We're halfway through debating on TV
And when we're interrupted, you propose

Instead of just rescheduling, I lock
My rival up in *jail*?

FLOURNOY.

> Not you. Police.

TAYLOR.

He's raised militia on the streets in full
And bloody insurrection 'gainst the state.
As former prosecutor you will see
The case could not be clearer. If he's left
Unpunished for this breach the law is dead.
A bloody coup permitted by us all.

FLOURNOY.

That law must be upheld, for if we flinch
As coarse rebellion engulfs our streets,
Then states will act where we do not, and claim
It's proof they need a new confederacy

HARRIS.

I think you all, that's *all* of you, just need
To take a moment. And you forget I'm not
Elected president, my mandate's weak

RICHETTI.

All those who voted Biden knew that you
Would sit a heartbeat from the president
And since his heart had nearly eighty years.
Your mandate's strong indeed.

Beat.

FLOURNOY.

Kamala. Every moment you delay
Increases the fatalities and with those dead
There's many missing too, we know not where.
Like Charlie Takahashi, he was out
Reporting, now the *New York Times* tells us
He's disappeared.

HARRIS.

> He's gone? But where? Is he

Okay?

FLOURNOY.
>Right now there's no one knows.
>The roads and city centres all are blocked
>With trucks whose drivers vet all those who wish
>To pass. In day the groups, they fly their flags, but with
>The setting sun they roam in shadow clans
>Violently pursuing those who might dissent.

>You need to shed the pond'rous shell of thought
>And learn that now you act. For when you do
>I promise then you'll sleep straight through the night.

HARRIS.
>We must find Charlie, and the rest.
>And stop the gangs.
>Enact the curfew now.

TAYLOR.
>Yes ma'am.

FLOURNOY.
>And what of Trump?

A moment.

HARRIS.
>Lock him up.

The loud sound of a jail door slamming shut.

4.3

Enter DON JR *and* ERIC, *at the Trump Washington residence.*
ERIC*'s playing a game on his phone.*

In the background, the sound of protest and marching.

ERIC.
>I'm very busy, tell me what you want.

DON JR.
>You've seen the daily crowds?

ERIC.
>I have. I tried to leave but then my own
>Security did hold me back and said
>That if I wanted burgers I would have
>To order in. They said the crowds were armed?

DON JR.
>They are. With nightly flames and rioting
>All this while shouting in our father's name.
>I fear that if this carries on, it won't
>Lead to a glorious vict'ry, but a rout.
>His name and ours will be forever shamed
>With streets of blood, and prosecution then
>Will follow, leading them to you and me.

ERIC.
>You think?

DON JR.
>   You don't?

ERIC.
>   Not much, but I don't want
>To go to jail.

DON JR.
>   Then listen well, for with
>Our father gone we have a chance to tell
>His deputy, our sister, that it has
>To stop.

Enter IVANKA.

>   My beauteous sister, how are you?
>What news of our incarcerated dad?

IVANKA.
>No news.

DON JR.
>   Alright, well seeing on TV
>And from my window, all the violent scenes,
>I'm worried, Eric too, it's got too much.
>And with our father put away there is
>A chance to say these fearsome gangs have served
>Their purpose and can now disperse

IVANKA.

    Our father's not away but in a cell.
    For on the doorstep set down fifteen cars
    And thirty officers, as if it was
    Goliath they did apprehend, and not
    A septuagenarian. It all
    Was theatre, and Dad complied at once.
    But still it is distortion of their powers.
    And Dad's made clear he wishes all the mobs
    Continue. If he stays in jail they are
    The presence he cannot provide himself.

DON JR.

    But we must think beyond his current aims.
    For if they prosecute, they will demand
    The full disclosure of our files and more,
    Great testament from those employed. There's none
    Of us within his circle who'd escape
    Examination by a crew most biased
    Towards their prejudicial law.

IVANKA.

                    You're scared.

DON JR.

    Uh-huh! You should be too! For only Dad
    Can pull the strings that mean he might survive.
    Without him we are toast.

Beat.

    And so I've had a meeting that, although
    Discreet and masked, was clear in its intent.
    The president herself conveys that if
    We do inform the FBI about
    Our father's often dubious dealings – all
    His finance, personal, political,
    With proof and records, testament in court
    To come, then in return whatever we
    Ourselves have done will get immunity.
    So any of our father's crimes will not
    Be visited upon his children.

IVANKA.
A meeting?

DON JR.
Yes, a conversation, yes

IVANKA.
Who set this conversation?

DON JR.
I've got five kids.

IVANKA.
And I have kids myself.

DON JR.
And I don't want their father put in jail.

IVANKA.
But yet their grandfather...

DON JR.
Will look out for
Himself.

A moment.

IVANKA.
Eric, you're on your brother's side?

ERIC.
I wouldn't thrive in jail.

IVANKA.
That's no doubt true.

IVANKA *makes a phone call.*

Please make a statement from our family.
To those out on the street who've nightly marched.
Our father offers thanks and loves them all
But now they should go home and wait to show
Their adoration through the vote instead.

DON JR.
I thank you sister, now we must move fast.
For any moment Dad might be released.
I have the presidential contact here.

We'll call and she'll arrange immediate
Protection of ourselves, and all our kin.

IVANKA.

Give me your phone.

DON JR.

You... want... Alright.

He hands the phone across.

IVANKA.

For it's your father's property, and if
You will betray his love you must reject
His gifts as well.

She puts his phone in her bag.

DON JR.

We... need to make the call.

IVANKA.

Your instinct 'bout the violent crowd's not wrong
They should be pacified, and do no good.

DON JR.

Indeed.

IVANKA.

But for the rest I have contempt.
Your father gave existence, nourished you
From birth, and scraped the watery shit from off
Your privileged ass. He gave you luxuries
You hadn't earned and education that
You don't deserve.

DON JR.

Ivanka, wait, we need –

IVANKA.

As adult he entrusted business that
He'd built for decades in your naive hands.
To let you sit atop a mound of gold
Yet with your shallow wife and children all,
You from that perch attempt to take a gun
And bring your father benefactor down

DON JR.

   He's been no father! None of that he's done
   Himself, he's outsourced everything, for us.
   From food, to school, to shit, to even love.
   We're ornaments to him. Possessions!

ERIC.

   It all was Don, for I am just, as well
   You know, a sniv'ling wreck with little sense.

IVANKA.

   Whatever brother. Your betrayal is most
   Complete, the call's been had, arranged
   And now your intermediary knows you're weak.
   And so this cruel decision will become
   Your death, in terms of access, money or
   Our dad. You're so tied up with him, I will
   Just type an email – I can do it now...

She produces her phone.

Just type the words and then press send –

DON JR.

                        Please don't.

She does.

IVANKA.

   And with that click, your assets fly away,
   Your access to all Trump material's
   Revoked, your precious correspondence wiped.
   I will secure a smallish house for each
   Of you, and families, and you will get
   A reasonable amount each year. But that
   Is it, and if you try to speak again
   To anyone about our father or
   Myself, that roof above your heads will go
   As well. Is all that clear?

Beat.

ERIC.

                   It is and thanks
   I do suspect I might be happier.

I've found all this has been too much, and now
The thought of just a house, and car appeals.

IVANKA.

I didn't say a car.

ERIC.

Okay, that's cool.

IVANKA.

And other brother? Well? What's your response?

DON JR.

This was our only opportunity
To make escape from out the darkness of
His overbearing hell. I love you still.
And still I think you know not what he is.

They go.

IVANKA.

Although they're right I find the violent mob
Unnecessary to achieve our ends,
I call them off to save my father not
Betray his trust. He plays a shorter game
Than I, he's more impulsive, more removed.
This means he sometimes lacks perspective, which
Is why he wanted me to be his hand.
And in his absence I will prove my point:
We will secure much greater victory from
Political attack, than allying
With rank and armed gangs we can't control.
Mine is a smarter route to power
We'll soar much higher than Trump Towers.

4.4

TRUMP *is sat on the floor of a prison cell.*

TRUMP.
>For God's sake, let us sit upon the ground
>And tell sad stories of the death of kings.
>How some have been deposed; some slain in war,
>Some haunted by the ghosts they have deposed;

>*Beat.*

>In fact for God's sake please let's not do that.
>Because from where I'm sitting they all sound
>Like losers.
>And though I might at first seem similar,
>Sat here imprisoned in this sullen cell,
>I'm not so sad, for shh! Here comes the secret;
>It's all the plan! For if you're smart it's not
>So difficult to guess how things play out.
>You cue a ball and playing well, before
>You strike, you'll know the end result. And so,
>When kept inside I'm instant made a martyr
>Arraigned like this, against my will, I'm turned
>The best recruiting sergeant for our cause.
>Already Dave my guard in here has put
>A picture of me on the floor onto
>His Instagram with an outraged emoji.
>Cos Dave's the biggest fan. He's beautiful.
>Hey Dave! How you doing?

DAVE, *the guard, opens the door and* HARRIS *comes into* TRUMP's *cell.*

>Oh.

DAVE *then goes.*

HARRIS *looks at* TRUMP *on the floor.*

HARRIS.
>Good morning Don. You know you've got a chair?

TRUMP.

But this is surely what you're after, no?
Your bitter rival bound and sadly gagged

HARRIS.

You're neither bound nor, sadly, gagged.

TRUMP.

But caged.

HARRIS.

Shall I explain our legal system?

TRUMP.

Sure.

That's all you ever do so go ahead.

HARRIS.

If you commit an act which breaks the law,
Police descend and hold you to account.

TRUMP.

You know I'm called unbeatable. Not true.
For if there were my doppelgänger, and
I ran against myself, I think I'd know
The ways to win.

HARRIS.

I've got some good ideas.

TRUMP.

But I don't think so. If you did, I doubt
I'd be in here –

HARRIS.

You've been arrested not
By me but the authorities

TRUMP.

You think
It's not within your power to release
Me from incarceration? Kamala! Come on!

Beat.

HARRIS.
   It's true. There's ways that I could have you freed.

TRUMP.
   Which actually you want. Each second that
   I'm locked in here makes you seem weak, and me,
   Take on a cool Mandela-feel. My long
   And lonely walk to freedom.

HARRIS.
                    How do you
   Imbue such hate in every syllable?
   You taint the very sounds with racist bile.

TRUMP.
   Don't know. It's natural. Like Mozart or
   That Lin-Manuel, Mike Pence he saw that show
   They called him out. So rude. He just sat there.
   I would have stood and answered back in turn
   And by the end the audience would have sung
   My shot not his, and changed the name that hung
   Outside from Hamilton to Trump.

HARRIS.
                    Now sir.
   Quite who do you amuse? There's no one here
   But me, and I'm not moved nor entertained.
   'Tis like you have an audience in your head
   And even when alone you do perform
   Your fantasy toward t'imagined crowd.
   Your whole psychology craves the applause.
   You see them now? The little people in
   Your raving mind?

TRUMP.
              I don't know what you mean.
   But I assume you're here to strike some deal
   My freedom, for assurance that I'll play
   According to your rules.

She produces a piece of paper.

HARRIS.

Disband in perpetuity your groups
Of armed men and women 'cross the states.
Your daughter has already ordered them
To leave the streets.

TRUMP.

She has?

HARRIS.

Indeed. But you
Must publicly make clear you want no force
Or violence in your name. And furthermore
Agree you will accept the outcome of
The fair and free election when it comes.
If you do this, then liberty is yours.
And if you don't it's ten to thirty years
For insurrection. Here's a pen.
If I were you, I'd sign your name.

She puts the paper on the floor with a pen.

Then she pulls up the chair and waits.

TRUMP *picks up the paper and looks at it.*

TRUMP.

You still don't get why they despise you all.
You think it's wealth. Or nepotism? No
I'm rich. And very nepotistic, so
It's not to do with that.

HARRIS.

Okay, just sign?

TRUMP.

You cannot understand why they all vote
For me. Can you? Well let me help you out:
It's that you say you listen but you don't.
You order them around. 'Hey don't own this!
Hey don't do that!' You speak to them like kids.
And not just kids but poorer less good-looking
Trashy kids, that you and your celebrities
All constant lecture, from your raised pile.

They stay on lowest wage while you reserve
Your fight for theory built in Ivy League.
For 'mental health' and *women* always women!
Meanwhile our tide was lifting all the ships
Around the world, the poor have risen from
Not owning bikes to choosing tariffs on
The latest phone. And by the way, the group
That's felt the benefit the most, guess what?
It's all the women, and that wasn't you, but us.
They want our country run
As thriving company not charity.

He suddenly shouts:

America Rules!

He listens. Echoed back to him, in the distance, they chant.

You hear that now? The inmates. What music!

I have my audience.

HARRIS.
    I made a clear decision years ago
    Because of what I saw, and what I lived
    To spend my life pursuing justice and
    In office I have always fought for people
    Who've been abandoned underneath the pile.
    From waking till I sleep I do my best.
    Even the ones who'd never put their mark
    Against my name, I fight for them as well.

    TRUMP *stands.*

TRUMP.
    Yet you don't trust them on the voting day
    To make a choice that benefits them best.
    Cos if you did, you wouldn't come with this,
    A smudgy contract clutched in blackmail hands,
    Instead you'd set your store within the vote

HARRIS.
    Electing you again would be the worst.

TRUMP.
    Okay but what if worst is what they want?

Chanting sound.

You want to know the way I'd be defeated?
Cos I can tell you, I don't mind at all?

HARRIS.
You gonna sign the thing or not?

TRUMP.
Why won't you ask to hear it? Simply pride?

A moment.

The first mistake was to impeach me twice.
Investigating dodgy Russian deals made sense
To sway some middle ground. But second time
We all had seen the footage of that day
And everyone already had their view.
So it appeared as soon as you had won
You made to stop near half the country from
Electing their man of choice. And then a ban
On Twitter, Facebook too, it seemed that all
The monsters of the swamp had risen up
Attempting to behead the people's choice
So to defeat me: first I would ensure
Debate was free, that silencing was not
An option. For that tactic reeks of fear.

HARRIS.
Not fear but law. A country cannot work
Without the legislation to protect
The mechanisms of the state –

TRUMP.
                    Okay,
I'm bored by that already, which in fact
Does lead me on unto my second point.
For when I'm running, every citizen
Who's got the vote can tell you what I'll do.
They all could name five things. So first time round:
The wall. The jobs. Iran. And Paris too.
We'll stop Obamacare. That's five right there.
But Hillary? You might remember that
She stood but not what she stood for. Hooray

She is a woman! That much we can see
But no one really knew the things she craved
Joe said he'd 'heal' and undo what I'd done.
But what of his? My rivals always fight
For how things *used to be*. Which doesn't set
The juices flowing in the voters' loins.
So Kamala, for Christ's sake stop the crap
About the goddam law and telling us
The ceilings through your race and gender smashed.
Instead work out what change you'd like to make.
That might drown out my nasty rhetoric
With glistening floods of sexy plans.

HARRIS.
It's like you want your own defeat.

TRUMP.
There's not much fun in only selling cars
To little ladies who'll pay sticker price.
I want a battle, blood and glorious war.
A vict'ry earned not seized and you –

HARRIS.
The crucial part is vict'ry. Your mouth
Is sloppy, makes one think the words it spits
Are careless, but in fact the aim's refined.
Relentlessly pursuing what you want.

TRUMP.
What do I want?

HARRIS.
                    To reinstate the policies
That civil rights undid, and preference whites
And men, and straight, and able-bodied folks
Before all others. More than that, you will,
Supported by your stacked high court, begin
To make consolidation of your power
Reduce the oversight, increase the reach
Of Oval Office, and in time, demand
Another term, on the basis that
There's nothing in the constitution that

Restricts it down to two, in fact that's just
A modern change, since nineteen fifty-one.

TRUMP.
And there you're right. What's done can be undone.

HARRIS.
And every term you win, your enemies
Are silenced and suppressed some more, until
There's no dissent at all, there's prison camps,
For those who question, riches in excess
For those who don't, and only older men
And women, will in quiet corners speak
Regretfully, now much too late, of what
They would have done, if they'd in time believed
That these United States could one day fall,
Despite the efforts of the Fathers,
Into a pair of most despotic hands.

TRUMP.
Our president is fantasist.

HARRIS.
                    No sir.
For every word of that is on the record
Directly from your most disgusting mouth.
Your idols are dictators. Many times
You've craved the power that they cruelly wield.

TRUMP.
You're an ugly person, sorry, but you are.

HARRIS.
You're lonely. You don't have a single friend.

                    You make your jokes upon
The stand for what can seem like days, at first
I couldn't get why you would waste your time
And then I saw it clear: No one but them
Will give you time of day.

TRUMP.
                    Oh no. Not true.

HARRIS.

> Your wife lives separately, your kids despise
> Your guts, and so you need a place to go
> Where you can simply talk.
> The lonely loser hates the world and so
> Resentful, turns his tantrums on us all.

TRUMP.

> You look at me and this is what you see?

HARRIS.

> It is. From crying wolf now many see
> A faded joke. But I perceive a clear
> And present danger, lethal and not funny.
> A bloody dog within our well-stocked farm.

He takes the paper.

TRUMP.

> Well then, my lady, lock the danger up.

He folds the paper and gives it back to her.

> You cannot have a predator set free.

A moment.

HARRIS.

> What did you do to Joe?

TRUMP.

> Just shook his hand.

HARRIS.

> And whispered something.

TRUMP.

> About his wife. A little thing.

> That's all it took.

> You see? It's possible to love too much.

A moment.

> What do you love Kamala?

A moment.

Then HARRIS *tears the contract up, goes and opens the door.*

She stands back.

HARRIS.
Imprisonment will only strengthen you
And in my core I must believe the people
All have their eyes to see, and mind enough
With conscience too, to know just what you are,
And having known, reject it out of hand.

TRUMP.
That's quite a risk.

HARRIS.
               No risk, for if I don't
Believe in that, then all my faith is gone.

TRUMP.
Well that's another thing to aim for then.

He leaves.

She stands alone in the cell.

HARRIS.
The Senator John Lewis wisely said
Democracy is not a state. Instead
It is an act. And this I understand.
Were't not for bold and unexpected deeds
Then I would not now be the president
Not even citizen, but caged and priced
My status that of property. So yes,
There's something must be done, but as to what…?
The leftist squad would blaze their weapons all
And want an all-out war. Then those like Joe
Expect that I should reach across the aisle
And tempt the moderate Republicans
To recognise that Trump serves not the state
But just himself. And yet the heady taste
Of victory sweetens all his bitter drugs
Intoxicating their support into
A selfish trance, which dims the side effects.

So none of these uncertain roads lead to
Success. And while incarceration may
Provide solution of pedantic Law,
Who stands upright in gown and wig with files
Of paper on her deftly ordered desk,
When creeping Realpolitik appears
He'll take a match of outrage to that ream,
Before it's read, and claim it all was lies.
A locked-up candidate does make a martyr.
So what is left? To stand aloft upon
The hill, in state, like all those statues that
Adorn the mall, as this most toxic flood
Engulfs our country with its thickened bile?
Who is this president? What can she do?
I fear that all the rules and principles
I've learned are meant for times of peace. And so,
Should acts in other times I would abhor,
Become my own, in times of bloody war?

ACT FIVE

5.1

Trump's Washington residence. Night. Rain outside.

TRUMP *enters. Looks around.*

Then IVANKA *enters separately.*

IVANKA.
My father you are walking free! The last
We heard they tried to strike a deal, which we
Of course refused.

TRUMP.
The president herself
Did call and try to make this deal. But she
As much as I, knew full well how it looked

IVANKA.
I'm glad that she at last saw sense.

TRUMP.
Me too.

Beat.

IVANKA.
And have you seen the news? Your glorious
Release is celebrated cross the world.
It's called a triumph for democracy.

TRUMP.
You're pleased?

IVANKA.
Of course.

TRUMP.
And you sued every day
In all the courts to grant my freedom, yes?

IVANKA.

Yes every day.

Beat.

TRUMP.

I hear you played the father and dispensed
Some justice to my wretched eldest sons.

IVANKA.

They were intending to betray your love
And sell their secrets to the Democrats.

TRUMP.

To me the punishment you handed out,
Sounds less like justice, more like mercy.
If I had found out what they meant to do,
I would have torn their coward guts away.
And I'm in fact surprised.

IVANKA.

By what?

TRUMP.

That as I came upon our house I thought
The streets would flow with crowds most jubilant.
That cheers would greet my journey from the jail.
But no, the roads were empty. Not a soul.

IVANKA.

Yes Father I –

TRUMP.

Upon enquiry,
I'm told that word went out to leaders 'cross
The nation telling them to dissipate
And wait at home instead. Then next week go
And meekly cast their vote.

IVANKA.

I sent that word.

TRUMP.

I've ordered their immediate return.

IVANKA.
Alright –

TRUMP.
                    Were my instructions hard to get?

IVANKA.
But you weren't here, and I assumed that when
You made me your vice-president-elect
You'd know I'd act according to my skills
My judgement so I assessed –

TRUMP.
You said your heart was strong.

IVANKA.
                              I did it not
Because I'm weak, but since they will not serve
Our purpose on election day –

TRUMP.
Our purpose on election day is strength.
I won't be hampered as before by rules.
The legal experts every way you turn.
In business my approach was charm combined
With fear. As president I had that charm
But lacked the lurking terror to achieve
The full extent. For all great leaders have
A ruthlessness the people grow to love,
Yes Thatcher, Churchill, Reagan, all the kings
From years ago Ivanka. Have you read
Machiavelli's *Prince*? I've not. It's long.
But someone summed it up, and it made sense.
And so I need the force, the guns, the thought
That voting for the other guy brings doom,
But put your mark by me and then be safe.

IVANKA.
Our polling showed that many undecided –

TRUMP.
I'll never hear another poll again.

IVANKA.

Well then what if we push them to command
The full resources of the state in ways –

TRUMP.

What have you done Ivanka, in your life,
To earn authority to lecture me
On how to win? To go against my clear
Desire, and take a dumb advantage of
My absence to impose your clumsy will?
It's arrogance extreme for –

IVANKA.

Not arrogance at all, I want you sat
Back in the office where –

TRUMP.

Let's be clear about
Just who you are Ivanka, since you seem
Deluded, like a toddling child, who dressed
Up as a nurse with plastic stethoscope
Believes she'll cure the deadliest of ills,
So you, most richly costumed in your suit
For business, sat upon my golden throne
Do think you are a deal. You're not. I'd hoped
By dressing as my heir, by standing close
And copying my style, you might acquire
My genius. But no.

IVANKA.

I've worked so hard –

TRUMP.

Maybe it's not your fault. You lack the balls.
The strength of will but also literally.
You lack testosterone, you think more on
Your kids, you're more agreeable, and not
Ambitious in the way we are. That's not
Opinion, all the science shows that's true.
I've always doubted that a woman could
Fulfil the role, which you have proved. You cry,
And look upset, and stamp your feet, and lack

A sense of humour, I can't talk to you
It's like I've got a child as second when
I need a proper grown-up there. A man.
If truth be told. No, no don't cry again –

IVANKA.
I'm not.

TRUMP.
You might, and I would have to hand
You to a functionary to sort that out,
Okay so not vice-president, it's not
The role for you, that's fine, well you can still
Inherit wealth, when that day comes, because
You are my daughter, comforting, and still
My little girl. But please forgive me if
I get a guy to do the actual job.
No, no, don't storm away, if that is what
You're stood considering, it simply will
Confirm the whole thing that I've said.

IVANKA.
I'm not.

I just ask that you reconsider. Though
Perhaps we don't agree about the way
We'll get the votes, I'm sure that if we talk,
We'll come to some agreement we can both –

TRUMP.
I don't employ the people sitting round
To force a watery compromise on each point.
And every point. Ivanka, you have shown
Me who you are. I'm disappointed. But
We'll all move on at speed, you'll be surprised.
Now I must eat. The food inside was such
A rancid pile of shit. Go find out what
They've got to bring me right this moment now.
I want to watch TV. Ensure my gangs
Are on the street and roaming up and down.
Those highways lead us to the oval crown.

He storms off.

She takes a moment to think.

Then, as she leaves, she gets out DON JR*'s mobile phone from her bag…*

5.2

The Oval Office. Night. Dim lighting. In the distance, the sound of fighting.

In the corner, a TV flickers – images of disaster. A low murmur of the news.

FLOURNOY, TAYLOR, *and others are there.*

Enter HARRIS. *She looks grave.*

HARRIS.
    Okay, I'm here, let's get the evening doom.

TAYLOR.
    The National Guard protects the centres of
    The government in all the troubled states.
    Policing leave's been cancelled but it's not
    Enough. The only areas with peace
    Resound with total praise for Donald Trump
    Or are suppressed and frightened, shuttered in
    Their boarded homes. It's said that many have
    In desperation hung a MAGA cap
    Outside their door, and like the cross for Moses,
    They hope the deathly curse will pass them by.

HARRIS.
    The curfew?

TAYLOR.
                    Unenforceable.

HARRIS.
                                            And my
    Appeals for calm –

FLOURNOY.
They fall on deafened ears.

HARRIS.
So what's the plan?

A moment.

Well? Surely you don't ask
Me here without an idea of the way?

TAYLOR.
In truth we fear the only course that's left.

FLOURNOY.
And you should fear it too.

HARRIS.

What course?

A moment where no one speaks.

An ATTENDANT *enters and gives* FLOURNOY *a piece of paper.*

ATTENDANT.
My Madam President, there is outside
A man insists he speak with you at once.
He has a valid pass and says you're friends

HARRIS.
His name?

FLOURNOY *reads further down.*

ATTENDANT.
It's Charlie Taka/hashi.

HARRIS.

Charlie? Found at last?
Well there's some joy! Let's hope that he
Can help untie our knotted state.

Enter CHARLIE, *with an* AIDE *leading him. He's wearing dark glasses.*

Well Charlie if I ever needed friends, it's now!
But why the glasses, why this woman as

Your guide? Come in. And now I'm closer, all
These wounds and bruises... what has happened here?

He takes off his glasses. His eyes are gone.

CHARLIE.
They found me out. And took me to some yard.
Removed all my possessions. Stripped my clothes.
And there applied some acid to my eyes.
They said because my occupation was
To spy, they'd take away my sight.

HARRIS.

But who?

CHARLIE.
Resentful men with spite turned violent,
Upon the streets unhindered by the law.
And I am not the worst atrocity.
In fact I'm lucky, still to be alive.

HARRIS.
We'll find the gang who did this. They will pay –

CHARLIE.
Maybe, if so then first you must restore
The courts, and find extra police, for those
On duty, worn and tired, are aware
There's little reinforcement now to come.
And even if one day you find those men
And lock them up... it's not a thing I'll see.

HARRIS.
Oh curse this Moderation in my soul!
This is your wav'ring fault. I've sought, in vain
A beast within to break my strict compassion
But now my friend who saw what most did not,
Is blind, and others dead, and in no time
We're facing a dictator in this place...
Charlie – we'll get you treatment, we can place
A man upon the moon, there must be ways
To here restore some light into your eyes!
What was the course unspoken?

TAYLOR *and* FLOURNOY *look at each other.*

Well?

You said a way you feared? And I should too.

TAYLOR.
When faced with allied countries falling prey
To tyranny, in ways that would not just
Curtail the human rights of their people
But be against the interests of our own,
We have been known to silently remove
The crucial piece from off the playing board.

HARRIS.
You know for just suggesting this I should
Take you to court.

TAYLOR.
                    Forgive me madam.
One cannot tend
An Eden without getting dirty hands.
I am a life Republican, and now
I know not where my party's gone. We don't
Conserve, or prize tradition but instead
Do seem intent on vandalising all
The principles that I hold in my heart.
I've fought on battlefields, and ended lives.
And when you do, you have to know the hill
On which you'd happ'ly die and this is mine.
I fight for freedom and that is not his aim.

HARRIS.
So what?

FLOURNOY.
            We have a way.

A moment.

You must have sometime thought, when learning how
The Nazis came to power, if back then,
You'd ended up sat close to him, and known
Somehow, the horror he'd inflict –

HARRIS.

It's not

The same

FLOURNOY.
And if, concealed within a pocket,
You had, somehow, a gun. Would you have raised
That pistol then, shot Adolf Hitler dead,
And saved the lives of millions?

Beat.

Well now
You're near enough, the weapon's in your hand.

HARRIS.
He is not Hitler.

FLOURNOY.
No
But every time the devil strikes he wears
A different face.

HARRIS.
We're talking like the vote has been played out
We should have faith in what the people see.

CHARLIE.
Unless he's forced them blind.

Beat.

FLOURNOY.
And Kamala I know your thoughts by now
And yes you're right. You do this thing your heart
Will break. You'll never look me in the eye,
Your conscience dead, your hands forever stained
In blood, not from a war, but hidden murder.
The end'll give no comfort from the means.
The price will be a crack within your soul
But that's the cost of sitting at the desk.

A moment. HARRIS *walks around the desk. Considering.*

HARRIS.
I say the word?

TAYLOR.

You do.

HARRIS.

What word is that?

TAYLOR.

Madam President. You make your wishes clear.

A moment.

HARRIS.

You have your hill, and I have mine.
I cannot take the people's choice away
For if I do, I will ensure there sits
A tyrant at that desk, but she will have
My name. And so I'll trust the people's vote.
I'm sorry both. And Charlie too. For yes,
I have my principles, and so, here as
The president, can never look
You in the eye and say I think that man
Must surely die.

Beat.

But yet I'll pray the Lord
May act where I cannot, and intervene
To end the suffering of our people soon.

FLOURNOY.

You'll... pray?

HARRIS.

Why Tina yes. For something like
The Hand of God to reach down to the earth
And with a cosmic justice only gods
Can wield, do deadly sin to guarantee
Our bliss.

They look at each other.

FLOURNOY.

Goodnight Madam President. Sleep well.

HARRIS.

Goodnight.

She goes.

As she does we hear the sound of a mobile phone… ringing in the distance…

…and the aide is revealed as ROSIE. ROSIE *watches them leave.*

5.3

Washington Trump compound. The same night.

TRUMP *enters, in military uniform.* IVANKA *follows, and* ATTENDANTS.

Also GUARDS, *all armed, standing to attention.*

TRUMP.
At ease.

The GUARDS *stand at ease.*

IVANKA.
I didn't see you in a uniform.

TRUMP.
Why not? For as the president before,
I'm commander-in-chief, and so if I
Must have the heavy burden of that role,
I ought to get to wear the costume too.
Oh yeah, and I got one for you, they had
Your measurements, it's out the back if you
Would like? A proper Private Benjamin.

IVANKA.
I'd rather not –

TRUMP.
                    Hey give me the gun

The SOLDIER *gives* TRUMP *the gun.*

I love a gun, I do. Bang! Right? You know
That time I said that I could shoot someone
On Fifth and get away with it? That's not
A joke, I really could. Right now, I could
Say, take this gun and hold it to the head
Of someone here –

He points it at IVANKA*'s head.*

              and pull the trigger. And
I promise you, that come election day
I'd still be on the ballot. And I'd win.

A moment.

Then he lowers the gun and gives it back to the SOLDIER.

Don't worry, it's a joke, okay? You know
I'd like to drive around our capital.
I'm sure they'd want to see their president
Bedecked in uniform.

IVANKA.
             I really would
Advise you not appear like that. Before
When you just wore an admiral's cap
So many veterans took against that look.

TRUMP.
But yet I am still here. You really think
Those vets want Joe or Kamala? Besides,
I think we're past that worry now. Next week
The booths will all be well-protected by
Our guys outside who'll offer help for folks
Who aren't sure how to vote.
But where's my favourite driver, what's her name?

IVANKA.
It's Rosie.

TRUMP.
        Rosie! Yeah. Go fetch her here.

Someone goes.

Come on Ivanka, dress as colonel now,
So we can go inspect our troops outside.
Remember in our first four years you were
Content as my advisor, so you should
Be happy in that most important role.
And smile! You bring the darkest fucking clouds.

Enter ROSIE.

Rosie, At last you're here! We want to tour
The neighbourhoods around DC, across
The town, from richest streets to ghettos too.
And you will drive us there, okay?

ROSIE.

Yes sir.

TRUMP.
And you –

He turns to the SOLDIER.

Accompany me within the car to give
Security but also we can look
And rate the girls who've come to grace the street
With their voluptuous support. Okay?
Perhaps they'll even join us in the car…

SOLDIER.
Yeah sir. That sounds amazing sir.

TRUMP.
Okay. Well Rosie get her fired up.

ROSIE.

Yes sir.

She turns to IVANKA. *Speaks quietly.* TRUMP *doesn't hear.*

I'll thank you madam. Farewell.

IVANKA.
My thanks to you. Your service will not be forgot.

ROSIE *goes.*

TRUMP.

Ivanka, still you're a civilian
You got a problem with the uniform?

IVANKA.

The uniform is wonderful, my thanks.
Unfortunately now I have to talk
To strategists and governors, who keep
The huge campaign on track. It is a lot.
And work that I suspect you'd rather leave
To me?

TRUMP.

That much is right. That sucks indeed.
You sit this out. Perhaps when I return
You'll put it on just once for me instead?

IVANKA.

Perhaps.

TRUMP.

Okay. Then let's go on parade.

IVANKA.

Wait, Father...

She goes and kisses him.

Though you never held me as
A child, disinterested by juvenile ways
And though I know I got things wrong, I'm still
So grateful for your rich inheritance

TRUMP.

Well sure, and when I die, you'll be amazed.
A whole lot more to come I promise you.

IVANKA.

My thanks, but on the day you finally rest
I'll make my thanks not for your bank account
But for a lesson learned.

TRUMP.

What lesson's that?

IVANKA.

That all relationships must be in play
And so in play, must there be played, to win.

TRUMP.

That's right. That lesson will bring you the world.
Before I go. Another kiss, my girl.

He kisses her again, then leaves with the troops.

She takes the uniform he's bought, produces a lighter and a cigarette from her pocket.

She lights the uniform so it catches fire.

As she watches it, she smokes the cigarette.

The sound of sirens.

5.4

A private hospital. 4 a.m.

VITA, *a nurse, enters, wheeling a gurney. On it is a figure, but with the number of masks and tubes, we can't see who it is.*

VITA *stands beside the trolley.*

VITA.

At night there's music.

All the beeping and pumping. Snores and groaning. When the going's good, it's got a rhythm. And since this is the best that money can buy, the most private, the best facilities, we try to keep things nice and calm. Beeping and pumping. Snores and groaning.

We only get the rich in here. I'm used to the circus that comes with that. The gold, the family, shouting and the endless stream of second opinions.

But you. Mister.

You are something else.

I mean how are you alive? Near eighty, severely overweight. I assume you've been pored over by the most expensive physicians every day of your life. Scanned and prodded and poked and first sign of anything they are in there and on it.

Until now.

Not much they can do about this.

Yet here you are. Still beeping. Still pumping. Still groaning in the night.

My mother was a wonderful woman. She loved cards. She'd sit and play her cards and as she played her cards she'd talk about sex. I don't know how much sex she had in the later days but in her youth from the sound of it she put the world to shame. And playing cards she'd relate the lot. It was, I have to say, an education. Then she got a cough, a temperature, she couldn't breathe, they took her away, and she died.

They say a lot of those deaths could have been avoided, if we'd worn the masks, and shut down better and earlier. And had a leader who made the difficult decisions. Still I forgave that, just. Maybe you didn't know. It's hard. Maybe even then, it would have happened whatever we did.

Until you got it. And you said you were strong, for beating it.

And I hated you then. Because saying you were strong meant you thought she was weak. And she was not. And while you were in the best bed money could buy, with your experimental treatments and doctors coming in and out, she went to a bed I don't know where and died with I don't know who. But certainly it wasn't where she loved or with who she loved.

And I'm not a doctor, but I've worked a while. And I know if I flick the switch to turn the power off, and if I remove the other machine, you will die, and there will be no sound to alert anyone, and I can switch them both back on, and you will be dead, and everyone round here will cheer, and say these things happen and everyone did their best, and I will not, I will NOT, get the blame.

I'm not afraid to say that in the night. With the music. My finger hovers over that switch. Because I could. I really could.

But I won't.

Because I won't give you the satisfaction.

To turn me into you.

For I am proud.

And you are not.

And Mom was proud.

And you are not.

And we are good.

And you are not.

SECURITY OFFICER *enters*. VITA *stands*.

HARRIS *enters*. SECURITY OFFICER *leaves*.

Oh my Jesus Christ.

HARRIS.
They didn't tell you I was coming?

VITA.
They certainly did not.

HARRIS.
Okay, well I apologise. It's for
Security I'm sure. They either make
The biggest deal or keep it a surprise.

VITA.
It's okay. I like you.

HARRIS.
I'm Kamala Harris.

VITA.
I know who you are Madam President.

HARRIS.
What's your name?

VITA.
  Vita.

HARRIS.
  Thanks Vita.

  Beat.

VITA.
  Okay. If you need me, press the button.

HARRIS.
  I will. And before you go, can you do me a favour? Wake
  him up?

VITA.
  I'm meant to keep him asleep.

HARRIS.
  I know but you got an injection or something that'll bring
  him round?

  Beat.

VITA.
  Sure.

HARRIS.
  Okay then.

  VITA *gets the injection and administers it.*

VITA.
  He'll take a moment.

  VITA *stands, then waits a second.*

  I'm gonna vote for you. When it's... When we can.

HARRIS.
  Thank you. Bye Vita.

VITA.
  Bye.

  She goes.

  HARRIS *presses a button and the bed raises up to reveal*
  TRUMP. *He is severely injured, on oxygen.*

He coughs, waking up.

HARRIS *takes off his mask.*

TRUMP.
Is she dead?

HARRIS.
The driver? Yes.

TRUMP.
Good.

Beat.

Where are the doctors? I've seen one guy.

HARRIS.
They checked if there was any extra funding, if you had insurance that could be claimed, but apparently your estate declined to provide. You're only here because it's easier for us to maintain security. But your care is what anyone else gets. The average American. No more. No less.

TRUMP.
You think I'm going to die?

HARRIS.
I don't know.

TRUMP.
I'm not.

HARRIS.
You crashed.

TRUMP.
You did it.

HARRIS.
An accident. Your driver.

TRUMP.
A spy.

HARRIS.
No. What I'm told?

Human error. Perhaps the road. The glare of the sun. No one's sure.

Essentially Donald, an Act of God.

You done anything that might upset him?

TRUMP.
    You want to gloat.

HARRIS.
    This doesn't make me happy.

    He looks at her.

TRUMP.
    I wish it did.

    Beat.

    What do the doctors say?

HARRIS.
    Your chances? Honestly? Not good.

TRUMP.
    Let's see. Where's Ivanka? You're stopping my visitors.

HARRIS.
    No.

TRUMP.
    I need to make a phone call.

HARRIS.
    You've got a phone.

TRUMP.
    Where?

HARRIS.
    On the desk.

TRUMP.
    I mean a real phone. My fucking cell.

HARRIS.
    Destroyed in the crash.

TRUMP.

Okay well – I don't know the numbers. Who knows the –
I've got no numbers I can't call anyone. You have to get –
Get me Ivanka on the phone!

HARRIS.

She knows you're here.

A moment.

TRUMP.

Get her.

HARRIS.

I am the President of the United States. I'm not the person
who fetches your daughter. Or your juice.

There's a nurse? But I don't know if you'll have much luck
with her.

Press the button.

A moment.

Then he does.

Nothing happens.

The beep of the heart monitor increases slightly in speed.

He presses the button again.

Still nothing.

The beep of the heart monitor increases a little more.

TRUMP.

You've told her not to come.

HARRIS.

She's busy.

A moment.

He catches his breath.

TRUMP.

So, not to gloat, and not to help.
Why come at all?

HARRIS.
>
> To say goodbye.

As president I have a duty
To the ghosts of all those federal executions.
To those who lost their lives the day the Capitol was stormed
And those within the last few weeks.
My friend made blind by your debase militia.
To all the victims of your policies.
These victims and their suffering
Will stuff your presidential library

TRUMP *struggles. Coughs.*

Your future's death.
And death's your only legacy.
That's if you're remembered at all

TRUMP.
I'll be remembered, after you and all
Your fellow mediocrities are dust

The heart monitor is rising again.

I'm not near death,
But ready for another decade, by
Which time I'll see you slumped upon your couch
Fatigued, and watching daytime news of me
Your president for life –

He's in pain. His breathing difficult. The monitor beeping fast.

That fucking nurse…

Oh –

(*To* HARRIS.) Five hundred.

HARRIS.
>
> What?

TRUMP.
>
> Five hundred… thousand.

To get the nurse. Save my life.

She looks at him. Doesn't move.

You greedy fucking –

Million.

Five hundred million to get the nurse.

HARRIS.
The button works.

So wait. Just wait, Don.

That's what the rest of us all have to do.

A moment, then he stands. Tears the wires off.

The heart monitor is a continuous noise now. Bits of him everywhere.

He stands. Triumphant that he can. Turns to HARRIS.

TRUMP.
An Act of God? No he bows down to me.
The Reaper is a loser. God? His son?
Just comfort for the huddled meek, who'll not
Despite the over-promising once made
Inherit any fucking thing at all.

He staggers towards the door, but his legs collapse.

He falls to the floor.

And dies.

HARRIS *reaches over and the steady tone stops.*

A moment.

Then VITA *enters.*

Looks at HARRIS.

And TRUMP.

VITA.
Oh.

He got out of bed?

HARRIS.
Couldn't stop him.

VITA *calmly checks the body.*

Then takes the sheet and puts it over the body.

VITA *and* HARRIS *exchange a look.*

VITA.
Paperwork.

HARRIS.
I bet.

VITA.
I'll get the porter.

VITA *leaves.*

A moment.

IVANKA *enters, in black.*

HARRIS.
He's gone.

IVANKA.
I know.

HARRIS.
Just now, he called for you.

IVANKA.
He did? I got the nurse to tell me when.

HARRIS.
So… when he called?

IVANKA.
When it was over.

Beat.

An Act of God.

HARRIS *looks at* IVANKA.

And yet already there's
These questions why I wasn't in the car
And why it was my driver that was used.

They say because now by default I am
The candidate, that I would gain from this.

HARRIS.

He didn't understand about his care
He thought there should be many doctors more
And nurses, treatments, no expense be spared.

IVANKA.

Despite his rhetoric he was so bad
With finance. Very bad. It made no sense.
On speaking with consultants here, to throw
Our money down the drain when he was gone
Or mostly gone. Instead we held it back.
And let him slip away.

HARRIS.

                      Alone.

IVANKA.

                      Which meant
He had around him at his death the sum
Of people that he truly cared about.

Beat.

My time as pretty woman on his arm
Is at an end. It served its purpose well.
And in due course, when polls are held, I will
Become this country's president-elect.
My father's death, I think you'll know, will not
Reduce my chances but will raise tenfold
The love I'll now be shown. And so, if you
As now you surely must, continue with
The free and fair elections, I will win.

HARRIS.

Okay. We'll see.

IVANKA.

                There's talk that it was you.
The driver was an agent of some sort,
Persuaded for her country's sake to crash.
And in a staged accident remove
Your problem from the ever-dark'ning plot.

HARRIS.
Your problem too.

IVANKA.
There's talk we did collude.

Beat.

HARRIS.
With any Act of God there'll be ideas.

IVANKA.
With JFK the circumstances caused
An everlasting murk. And if I may,
I doubt there'll be much reason to invest
In an inquiry too soon.

HARRIS.
                    Agreed.
We have more urgent matters.

Beat.

It isn't down to me, but if I'm asked.
I'll recommend election day comes soon.
The people are divided and require
Some kind of public resolution.

IVANKA.
                    Good.
We will with bated breath, await their choice.

She looks at her father.

Stands.

Then takes a breath.

It's beautiful that smell. So beautiful.

HARRIS.
What smell?

IVANKA.
                    Oh Kamala! Of freedom.

She goes.

HARRIS.
> A looming cloud, which dark and ominous
> Had blocked the sun, does now at last make way.
> I'd hoped we'd finally see some light, but yet,
> Another seems to follow in its wake
> With equal prospect of wild storms to come,
> So having fought to end the father's war.
> Should I have feared his daughter more?

End of play.

www.nickhernbooks.co.uk

facebook.com/nickhernbooks

twitter.com/nickhernbooks